Praise for
THE RECONSTRUCTING OF YOUR MIND

"Whether it's rebuilding demolished Temples, devastated cities, or deconstructed faith, the Bible has much to say about 'reconstruction.' For such a major gospel theme, these are the days for authentic memoirs and thoughtful manuals that walk us through spiritual upheaval. I wouldn't entrust my heart or yours to trendy cynics drunk on demolition. I commend to you my friend, Todd Vick, a fearless and seasoned guide whose work herein is both wise and accessible."

DR. BRAD JERSAK
DEAN OF THEOLOGY & CULTURE, ST. STEPHEN'S UNIVERSITY

"Using conversational language that makes for easy reading, Todd Vick gets at the heart of what troubles so many. What has come to be called 'deconstruction' is a journey with significant confusion and pain. Allowing for diverse experiences and expressions, this book offers an honest account of life with and without faith … with the possibility of a new faith."

THOMAS JAY OORD
AUTHOR OF *GOD CAN'T* AND *OPEN AND RELATIONAL THEOLOGY*

"*The Reconstructing of Your Mind* poses the question, 'What if the Great Commission is only really about love?' Todd Vick invites you to follow him on the spiritual journey that brought him to that conclusion. The book is a quantum leap backwards in the name of exploring the earliest church from a cultural perspective to reveal the heart of Jesus, all while engaging the reader with real, raw—and above all else—relatable stories from his well-trod journey. It lays bare the intent of the Gospel, while giving you all the feels. Todd helps Christians who have taken apart their faith rebuild a fresh foundation of hope, in the realization that 2,000 years of auxiliary theology cannot come close to representing the intent of Christ. Reconstructing your faith feels a lot like becoming the Phoenix rising from the ashes, something Todd captures perfectly. The book is a warm conversation about awakening from a staid slumber of the spirit. It is written from the perspective Christian who has questioned his faith and found it indeed strong, like that old rugged cross—roughhewn and solid—and built to last through our doubts and epiphanies. I cannot recommend *The Reconstructing of Your Mind* highly enough."

JANA GREENE
BLOGGER AND AUTHOR OF *FIERCE RECOVERY: LIVING YOUR BEST SOBER LIFE NOW* AND *EDGEWISE: PLUNGING OFF THE BRINK OF A DRINK AND I TO THE LOVE OF GOD*

"Reconstruction itself is a reckless pursuit. It's reckless because it is uncertain. It forces us to confront reality and to look beyond into an ever-expanding, unending universe. It's a reckless endeavor as we reach out into the void to touch what we cannot see. Jesus was a reckless lover. He pursued the people society had deemed irrelevant. He saw their relevance. Jesus saw into their hearts by way of intimacy and he penetrated them with grace. Reckless love is redemptive. *The Reconstructing of Your Mind* is about a redeemed relationship—with God, with the self, and with the neighbor. A redeemed relationship is intimate, diverse, and multi-dimensional. Todd's conceptualization of reconstruction incorporates the necessary attributes of redeemed relationships and practices for Jesus level compassion. His reckless words will captivate and encourage readers to confront cognitive challenges while reaching out toward what is real. For a fulfilling and reckless reconstruction, let this book be your guide."

DANIELLE KINGSTROM
WRITER AND HOST OF THE *RECORDED CONVERSATIONS* PODCAST

"With the heart of a pastor and the presence of a friend with whom you're having coffee, Todd joins you on the religious deconstruction journey in this book. Each page gives language and next steps toward one's total spiritual reconstruction. So thankful to have his unique timbre in the choir of other Reconstruction/Deconstruction voices."

MEGGIE LEE CALVIN
PODCASTER AND BESTSELLING AUTHOR OF *I AM MY OWN SANCTUARY: HOW A RECOVERING AUTHOR FOUND HEALING AND POWER*

"As death is necessary to resurrection, so is the death of religious thinking to deconstruction and deconstruction to reconstruction. In *The Reconstructing of Your Mind*, Todd Vick takes through his journey through deconstruction and reconstruction. Simultaneously scholarly and conversational, this book takes the reader by the hand and leads them through this often painful but always rewarding experience. Rich with scriptural, empirical, and anecdotal references, Todd not only encourages the reader to take the leap into spiritual deconstruction but also helps them to build wings that will enable them to both soar through the experience but also to give them a safe landing. Todd reminds the reader, at every turn, that (s)he is loved and valued and that they and their experience are both unique and precious. This book helps deconstruct deconstruction, resurrect reconstruction, and gives a healthy reality check to all things church—all with a heaping helping of the Love of Jesus."

DERRICK DAY
AUTHOR, SPEAKER, AND PODCASTER

The RECONSTRUCTING of your MIND

A POST-DECONSTRUCTION JOURNEY

TODD R. VICK

All rights reserved. No part of this book may be used or reproduced, stored in a retrieval system, or transmitted in any form or by any means, electronic, mechanical, photocopying, recording, scanning, or otherwise, without written permission from the publisher except in the case of brief quotations embodied in critical articles and reviews. Permission for wider usage of this material can be obtained through Quoir by emailing permission@quoir.com.

Copyright © 2021 by Quoir.

Cover design and layout by Rafael Polendo (polendo.net)

First Edition

Unless otherwise noted, all scripture quotations are taken from the Scripture quotations are from the ESV® Bible (The Holy Bible, English Standard Version®), copyright © 2001 by Crossway Bibles, a publishing ministry of Good News Publishers. Used by permission. All rights reserved.

ISBN 978-1-938480-88-1

This volume is printed on acid free paper and meets ANSI Z39.48 standards.

Printed in the United States of America

Published by Quoir
Oak Glen, California
www.quoir.com

DEDICATION

For Rachel

ACKNOWLEDGEMENTS

This book was intimidating for me to write. Reconstruction is a subject I have never written or preached about before. There are several friends, podcasters, and fellow authors who have inspired and encouraged me on my decon/recon journey: Jason Elam, Keith Giles, Chris Kratzer, Seth Price, Cody and Elaine Johnston, Karl and Laura Forehand, Michele Snyder, Meg Calvin, Brad Jersak, Danielle Kingstrom, Sean McCoy, Jon Turney, Wm. Paul Young, and the late Rachel Held Evans, to whom this book is dedicated. I hope this book of mine inspires someone as much as your friendship and books have inspired me!

I want to convey heartfelt gratitude to Dr. Andrew Newburg, a man of faith and a brilliant neuroscientist who examines the brains reactions to faith expressions. Your work is incredible, and I have learned so much from you!

I owe much gratitude to Rafael Polendo and the editors at Quoir Publishing. Thank you for including my work with the roster of amazing authors who push the boundaries of faith and religion seeking a more Christ-like way to live.

My family is my perpetual "why." You are why I do what I do. I want to help create a better world for you all. My beautiful grandchildren have brought a joy into my life that I never imagined possible!

Jesus, you are the absolute love of my life. When I had no one else, I always had you. At my worst, you were there. At my best, you were there. No one loves me like you do. I want to always decrease so you can always increase in my life, family, teaching, and writing.

CONTENTS

Foreword 13
Preface 17

Part One: The Teardown
1. The Deconstruction Dilemma 23
2. The Pesky Perception Problem 33
3. The Cognition Conundrum 39
4. The Cash Cow Confusion 45
5. Rebel Without Applause 51

Part Two: The Reframing
6. The Rocky Road of Reconstruction 57
7. Love, Death, and Resurrection 63
8. The Collapse of Community 71
9. The Fallacious Fear Factor 81
10. The Power of Presence 91

Part Three: The Reconstructing
11. Clean, Called, and Commissioned 103
12. The Great Commission Christian 111
13. Shepherds, Sheep, Souls, and Surgeries 119
14. The Velvet Jesus Painting 127
15. Reconstructing Your Personal Vision 137

Parting Thoughts: Where Do We Go From Here? 145
Appendix 149

FOREWORD

Deconstructing your faith isn't easy. In fact, it's probably one of the most painful seasons of life anyone could ever go through.

You probably already know this. It's probably why you're reading this book right now, I'm guessing. If so, you've made a wise choice. My friend, Todd Vick, understands how painful it can be to deconstruct your faith. He's not afraid to show you his scars, or to tell you the stories of how he got them.

That's one of the things I love most about Todd. He's painfully and sometimes almost uncomfortably honest. But this sort of honesty is so rare in our world today. It's very beautiful and refreshing to meet someone like Todd; someone who isn't afraid to tell you the truth, even when it hurts.

What I believe you will appreciate most about this book is that it is not only filled with real-world examples of how painful deconstruction can be, it's also filled with a lot of hope. In fact, if these true stories of rejection, loss, grief and deep spiritual trauma weren't followed by an equal number of stories about how Todd found a way through this pain, and fought his way back into the light again, it would hardly be worth reading.

Because we all have our own stories to tell, don't we? We all know how much it hurts to be rejected by our family, our friends, our church fellowship and even strangers on the internet over differences in theology. We really don't need any more proof of how much it hurts to question our faith, do we? No, we don't.

But what I do believe we need is what Todd has taken great care to provide us with and that's a healthy dose of hope to carry us through our darkness.

Now, as painful as deconstruction is, the reconstruction of our faith can be almost as difficult. At least, at first. But, unlike the deconstruction process that leads us out of certainty and into the wilderness of doubt, the reconstruction process is one we must undergo with great intention.

See, the process of deconstruction is mostly something that happens to us. We start to question something about our faith and as we begin to investigate and question it, we find ourselves seeing things we can't unsee and knowing things we can never un-know. It's probably why they call it the "slippery slope" because, once you start to ask these sorts of questions, the drop off is steep and the next thing you know you've got a dozen more questions to ask.

Deconstruction sort of just happens to us. But for those who want to take the next steps into reconstructing faith, there is something important to know right up front: It's going to take a lot of effort.

In other words, no one ever falls into reconstruction. Without an intentional, daily commitment to seek out a foundation for our reconstruction process, we'll never make it. Without a firm resolve to continually work our way towards a more hopeful way of living out our faith, we'll just keep spinning our wheels.

Reconstruction is hard work. There's just no easy way around it, my friend.

But here's the good news: in this book, my friend Todd Vick shows us how to do it. He lets us see how he made his way out of the wilderness of doubt and into the new frontier of spiritual reconstruction.

As you'll see, it's not a simple process. It takes courage. It involves a strong desire to move forward. It will take the rest of your life to get there. But as you begin to walk this road, you'll discover a few wonderful truths: God is good. God will never leave you. You are loved. And what's more, you are not alone.

If you decide to take the first step, this book will become a helpful source of hope and light for your journey. If you keep at it, you'll soon discover it's more than worth it to keep on going. Eventually, you will find yourself turning around to offer wisdom, strength, and hope to those who are coming up the road behind you. That's how it works.

I know you're eager to get started. I know you can do it. I'll be looking over my shoulder to see you coming up the road the rest of us have already travelled. It's going to be ok.

– **Keith Giles**
Author of *Jesus Unexpected: How the End Times Ended and Jesus Already Returned*

PREFACE

I had hoped to travel the world more by the time I reached fifty-two. My journeys thus far have been mostly spiritual. There have been many forks in the road on this journey. Each time I stopped at the fork I had a crisis of faith, followed by a choice of which road to travel. Every decision I made, even the difficult, heartbreaking ones, brought me exactly to the place where I am now. I recently completed the faith journey known as *deconstruction*. Now I realize that the title of the book lends itself to *reconstruction,* but to better understand this concept, we need to examine deconstruction.

Deconstruction as it pertains to faith generally means to question every single facet of one's belief system until there is basically nothing left. Every deconstruction experience is unique to the individual. Some of us grew up in the conservative faith tradition and were even educated by it. Some of us are (or used to be) pastors. Some of us are just high-brained people who see beyond the *because God said so* approach to faith and practice. God said it, that settles it, and they believe it ... but not if they are deconstructing. Everything you have ever believed about God, Jesus, the Bible, Heaven, Hell, the Rapture, the Second Coming, and Evangelism has come crashing down because you can no longer get behind it as it is. The common word for this is *deconstruction.*

There are at least 5 different types of Deconstruction:

1. **Religious Deconstruction**: For those who are weary of man-made religion and the restrictions it places on us.

2. **Theological Deconstruction**: For those who have been immersed in theological doctrine and dogma for so long that it has replaced simple and sincere faith.

3. **Biblical Deconstruction**: For those who dare to question the inerrancy of Scripture and its efficacy in modern culture.

4. **Church Deconstruction**: For those that are tired of going to a building every week to worship God, who needs no structure to contain him. And for those who have been hurt by the institution of Church.

5. **Faith Deconstruction**: For those (like me) who walked away from all the above, as well as belief in the divine at all.

We could probably create a bigger list if we needed to. To the Christian in deconstruction, or *decon,* your faith and practice just doesn't make sense anymore. You feel alone in a way that catches you by surprise. You feel guilty for questioning the things which have been indoctrinated into you all your life. You feel isolated from what was once your church family. Your blood family doesn't understand or even like what you're going through. *God's word is the final authority,* they warn you. You are afraid to deviate from what the Bible says. Adam and Eve questioned God's word. Afterward they were isolated and hiding. It's a scary thing to question everything you have ever believed and even more scary to walk away from it.

Decon feels like divorce. The person you committed to spend your life with tells you they are no longer in love with you, or that they just don't want to be married to you any longer. With that comes the unspeakable feeling of rejection followed by an unraveling of your beliefs about the institution of marriage. The two who were supposed to be one flesh are now two fleshes again. There is no emotional pain quite like it. When you decon, it is like a divorce. The Jesus you grew up with suddenly ceases to exist, at least in how you thought of him. Church that was a major part of your life suddenly isn't there anymore.

Decon is lonely, my friend. Questions like, *was there ever a God at all?* cause you some sleepless nights. *Was any of it real?* is another rough one. You recall the moments in prayer, worship, or youth camp where God really seemed to move in your life and wonder if it was just your imagination. Take heart...all of this does get better in time. However, you must first embrace the deconstruction dilemma. You'll be glad you did. I promise you that.

My first book, *The Renewing of Your Mind*, was an attempt to share my deconstruction journey. At the time I wrote it, I had never heard the word *deconstruction* regarding faith. I called it the renewing of the mind based on Romans 12:2. Whatever parts of my faith felt like a burden or were motivated by shame and guilt I ejected. I now seek a faith that spreads joy, love, and grace. I want to be a conduit of the authentic Jesus. I share a little more of that journey in Chapter One.

In this book, I wanted to lead you through my journey of *reconstruction*. To me it was a sometimes-painful process of rebuilding the structure of my beliefs into something that is not only more realistic but also extremely joyful! Your journey won't look like mine. Not exactly. You will also note that deconstruction/reconstruction occurs over and over. It's not a one-stop shop.

This book is divided into three parts. Part One focuses on deconstruction. Part Two begins the reframing process, and Part Three paints the picture of a reconstructed believer.

Again, your journey will look different than mine. It should. You're not me, you're you! My hope is that something from my journey will encourage you in yours.

Thank you so much for reading this book. It was a labor of love just for you.

– **Todd R. Vick**
Lexington, South Carolina
2020

Part One
THE TEARDOWN

Chapter One
THE DECONSTRUCTION DILEMMA

"Religion is the safest place to hide from God."
- FATHER RICHARD ROHR

For as long as I can remember, I have believed in God. As a child, God was the imaginary friend who rewarded good and punished bad. My belief system consisted of finding ways to be good and not bad. As I got older, my earthly father chose alcoholism over his family. If God was my heavenly father, then it was just a matter of time before he abandoned me too, or so I surmised.

On the 70s TV show, *Happy Days,* Fonzie, played by Henry Winkler, would occasionally remind God that he was his favorite. I wondered if God really did have favorites. If so, could I be one of them? How could I make that happen? I tried bargaining.

"Hey God, if I study hard for my test, will you help me get an A?"

"God, if you'll not let my Mom find out about me lying, I will be extra good this week."

My spiritual journey really began in my freshman year of high school. One day in gym, this guy with braces and large super-nerd glasses approached and introduced himself. For a nerdy guy, he was noticeably confident and comfortable in his skin. I liked him right away. His name was Rick Stilwell. My lifelong pal Jay and I have nicknames for just about everyone we know. We called Rick, *Rickwell.* That became his nickname among our whole group of friends. Mine was *Frog* (Todd = Toad = Frog). A few longtime friends still address me as Frog to this very day. Having a nickname was a rite of passage in our group.

It was Rick who not only invited me to his church but also came and picked me up. My first ever visit to a Southern Baptist church was at Trinity Baptist in Cayce, SC. There was a revival service going on. My first. The evangelist kept talking about being *born again* and having a *personal relationship* with God through Jesus Christ his only son. This was all new to me, and I really wanted that personal relationship with God. I had always believed in him, but I never really knew him. During the invitation/altar call, I went forward. Something had really stirred my heart that night.

The next thing I knew, I was carted off backstage and placed with a very scary old man who made me read out loud a tract called *The Four Spiritual Laws*. I was not comfortable at all. If this is what it meant to know God, maybe I was better off not knowing him. The scary man finally let me go. Then the evening got even more weird. When I returned to the sanctuary, total strangers were hugging me and patting my back. They congratulated me for becoming a Christian. I had become a *Christian?* I had thought I already was one. I was so confused. All I wanted to do was go home. As unpleasant as home was, it was far better than scary old men and pseudo-happy strangers.

The next day, I told Rick how I felt, and he was so cool about it. He encouraged me to at least try going with him to Sunday School. I never understood the purpose of Sunday School, quite frankly. Monday through Friday school was plenty for me. I quickly discovered, however, that my life was about to change in a big way.

The following Sunday, I was introduced to my Sunday School teacher, Frank Ward. I had never met anyone like him before. His lessons were so easy to understand and quite challenging. He spent a lot of individual time with me answering my many questions about the Christian faith and this business of having a personal relationship with Jesus. He genuinely cared about me. When I ran out of questions, Frank encouraged me to make a commitment to follow Jesus. On Saturday, April 11, 1983, I prayed the sinner's prayer along with Frank. The next day I joined the church as a full-fledged member. Two weeks later, I was baptized by immersion. I stayed there for eleven years, I was saved and baptized there. I got married there. I dedicated my firstborn there.

I could write entire volumes about my experiences there and the many friendships I made and still enjoy all these years later. Rick was one of my dearest friends for thirty years. Over those years, he and I had many conversations about the state of Christianity. When I graduated Bible College, he and I had taken different theological paths. I was the staunch conservative, and he was more progressive. We both respected our journeys, even though I was kind of an ass about *my* theology. Rick and I always disagreed agreeably even when I was being a legalistic ass. He was reading Brian McLaren's *A New Kind of Christian* at the time. I was convinced that the old kind of Christian was more than sufficient. I have since read McLaren's books and wish that I could tell Rick what a fool I was.

Rick died very suddenly in January of 2013. The loss is still raw; the void he left is still there. It always will be. I dedicated my first book to him. It was inspired by our years of meaningful conversations about grace and theology. He had also tried to get me to read books by Rob Bell, Leonard Sweet, and several others. Being the conservative that I was, I politely passed. Our last conversation was so good that I took notes! Rick was years ahead of the rest of us. He was a deep thinker. He loved Jesus. He loved the Church despite her flaws and shortcomings. He was an amazing husband and father. He was a faithful and steady friend. I always knew he was there for me, no matter what. After his death, his friends and colleagues created a hashtag just for him, *#livelikerick*. That was his legacy. He lived like Jesus. He was someone whose life inspired so many people all over the world. He was a social media expert. He had friends all over the world, many of whom he had never met in real life, but they loved and admired him just the same. That is the miracle of social media and the connections it affords. He believed strongly in connection … intimate, meaningful, human connection…over coffee when possible. He championed both caffeination and connection.

As I draft this book, it has been seven years since Rick passed away. I miss him profoundly. He was a very stabilizing presence in my life. He believed that questions could be more valuable than answers. He was all about growing and evolving spiritually and as a man. He was the first person to model deconstruction for me. Neither of us were familiar with the term, but there was no doubt that Rick was a true deconstructionist whether he knew it or not.

THE MINISTRY DECONSTRUCTION YEARS

At age sixteen, I was "called" vocationally to the ministry. I started out the ministry by teaching Sunday School, singing, visiting prisoners, and youth camp counseling. Later I was a minister of music and youth at a couple of churches in North and South Carolina. I decided to finish my college degree at Southeastern Baptist Theological College in Wake Forest, NC. When I was a student, we had four to five-hundred people on campus. Today it is at least five times larger! My classes were intimate—less than thirty people per class. I made some wonderful friends who challenged and cared for me. I lived on campus, mostly worked on campus, and seldom got out of Wake Forest. I was in a Southern Baptist "bubble," in which I was indoctrinated in the authority of God's holy, inerrant word, the Bible.

I learned biblical Greek and Hebrew. I was never an expert at either language, but I learned how to use my lexicons. I learned to be an expository preacher. I also learned arrogance. Maybe it was already there, but it really took shape in Bible College.

By the end of my first semester, I wanted to quit. I felt that I didn't belong there. When one receives a vocational ministry calling, it is an amazing feeling. I arrived at the seminary campus thinking I was going to be the next Billy Graham. That didn't last long. I thought I knew so much about God, Jesus, the Bible, and theology in general. Very quickly, I realized how over my head I was. I didn't understand why I had uprooted my family and moved to Wake Forest. I thought I would make a terrible pastor. Many of my friends and classmates were already pastors. They were (and still are) some amazing people. I felt like a blind man at a staring contest. I was unworthy of my calling in my mind. I wanted to go back home. One of my favorite professors and some good friends talked me through my first semester crisis, and I decided to stay and finish my conservative evangelical education and indoctrination with great humility. I graduated two years later and embarked on a thirty-year journey of pastoral ministry.

Almost all of my life, I wanted to be someone else. This mindset started as a child. Everybody I knew had a better life than I did. They had both parents, nice families, and nice homes. My father was an alcoholic and emotionally closed off. After they divorced, my mother was always tired from working to support my two sisters and I with no help from him. He abandoned us. Because of this, I always felt odd. My closest friends had good fathers, and I had no one. I never believed in myself, even when I was doing good or winning awards. I still felt less than everyone else. I think I overcompensated by trying to be the best at everything I did. Even when I succeeded, I still had a low opinion of myself. I had no faith in myself. This mindset followed me as a young man, a husband, a father, and employee, and later as a pastor.

I never trusted myself to be a good pastor, so I tried to emulate other prominent Baptist pastors who I admired, like Charles Stanley, Johnny Hunt, John MacArthur, and Tom Elliff. I studied these men and tried to be them. I even preached some of their sermons. I did Wednesday night Bible studies straight from MacArthur's commentaries. I couldn't remember the last time I had had an original thought of my own. Why? Because I didn't trust myself to lead as a husband, father, or pastor; I expected to fail, so I tried to become other people who I believed were way better than me so that I could be successful like them. They weren't always real people, either. I picked characters from television and movies to become. I was never enough as myself. I tried to live other peoples' lives. When I had my mental breakdown in 2016, I had no idea who I was. It had never even occurred to me to just be myself! Not one in my entire life did I just try to be Todd.

As a Christian, I simply tried to act like the people at church that I looked up to. I became good at wearing my church mask. My life at home was difficult, so I spent as much time away from there as I could growing up. I had about five surrogate families during high school. I seldom had people over to my house. I never wanted them to know how dysfunctional my life really was.

It wasn't until 2016 when I went to intensive outpatient psychiatric therapy that I discovered who Todd really was: a big mess. At the time I was in my final pastorate and couldn't give the church what they needed. My heart wasn't in it at all. I asked myself why, and I realized that I wasn't even sure I believed in God anymore. What good is a Christian pastor who doesn't know if he even believes in Jesus? Did I ever? Or was I just trying to be accepted by my friends? Those were hard questions, and that is way understating it. Everything I believed, everything I thought I was, and everything I had known since high school, was suddenly gone. It was like the death of an old friend. I knew exactly what that felt like. I thought about Rick more than ever. *How was he so comfortable in his skin? Why wasn't I?*

After he died, I began to seriously ponder my life as I compared it to his. He left an amazing legacy to his family and friends. I had hurt my family and friends. I didn't know at the time that I was entrenched in severe anxiety and depression. I loathed myself so much that I sabotaged every good thing in my life.

When the spiritual rug of your life is yanked out from underneath you, it is perfectly normal to go into crisis mode. Something was terribly wrong with me. I had lost my faith. The very thing that I devoted my life to sharing was just … gone. I was terrified. The fact of the matter is that I was more relieved than sad. I felt free—a lifelong burden had been removed from my sagging spiritual shoulders. If I didn't want to, I never had to go back to church ever again. *Let them have it!* I thought. I'm done. I'm out. The problem for me was that I no longer had a belief system. I am a spiritual-minded person. I needed *something* to grab hold of.

Before I left the church, I had acquired a job at a local furniture store. The owner and his family were Christians, but much different than what I was used to. They treated me like family from day one. I was doing really good there, and after a few months, a position opened in another store. This store was a one-man operation, as there was nowhere near the foot traffic than at my store. The owners had been so good to me and I didn't want to let them down.

At the new store, there was literally nothing to do for most of the day except sit at the computer in the office. I played on social media and binge-watched several series I had been wanting to see. I watched old movies I had never seen. Mostly, I watched things that pushed me out of my comfort zone. Every now and then, a customer would come in and I would stop and wait on them. I made some good sales, so the owners didn't mind me sitting at the PC most of the day. It was a great time of mental unwinding for me. I didn't have to focus on much at all. I was getting paid to use the computer pretty much. It was a healing time for me.

I soon became bored with binge-watching. I started to think about faith again. I felt empty inside, even though my life was good. I took to the internet exploring beliefs and why we need them. I connected with an amazing Hindu swami, who was so full of wisdom and kindness. He even suggested that Hinduism was not for me. He said that Christianity is where my heart belonged. I felt a little put off at the time, but now I realize what an amazing thing Swami J did for me. I began to read books by John Assaraf, Vishen Lakhiani of *MindValley.com*, and I discovered books on the brain and faith by Dr. Andrew Newburg.

I spent hours in front of the company computer watching Masterclasses taught by some incredible people I had never heard of before. John Assaraf's *Brain-A-Thon* was also one of my favorite things to watch. John has met with brain experts all over the world. His teachings about the brain are geared toward living the life you dreamed of by unlocking yourself from unhealthy beliefs and traditions that have held you back. I was taking pages of notes and absorbing as much as I could from these incredible people. I started writing *The Renewing of Your Mind* during this time. It took me three years and several rewrites to complete. Plus, there was so much research that I had done. The book didn't feel right to me. I felt like I was sharing information that had already been shared by John, Vishen, Swami

J, and others. It wasn't *my* book. I wasn't using my own voice. I was going back to trying to be these people rather than myself again. I wanted to write my own book. Something was missing, however. Or rather, some*one*.

Jesus. Not the Jesus I had been preaching for so long. Not the Jesus that I could do nothing but fail. Not the Jesus who sits at the right hand of God, shaking his disappointed head at me.

I wanted to rediscover the Jesus I met in 1983 as a teenager. Those first months as a Christian were like a dream. I talked to Jesus and he talked to me … like a brother. I wanted everyone to know him. I didn't understand how I ever lived without him. I walked on clouds during that time in 1983. Nothing bothered me because I had Jesus in my life. I also had some of the best friends in all of explored space. I was the happiest I had ever been!

Until … one day when I was sixteen years old. Something happened that forever changed me.

The scary guy that I mentioned earlier from the revival and his surprisingly sweet wife approached me after church one Sunday. They asked if they could talk to me for a moment. I said okay. They told me they had been praying for me and that God wanted them to tell me that I really shouldn't wear blue jeans to church. In 1983, I had two pairs of jeans. One with holes that I wore to school, and one pair without holes that I wore to church.

They also proceeded to tell me that God didn't approve of my long hair (my mane in my younger years was legendary!). They said it drew attention to me and not Jesus. Flummoxed and sick to my stomach, I thanked them and went home. I believed them. I was doing it wrong. I thought Jesus was pleased with me, but I was wrong. How dare I be so casual with the savior of mankind? I got a job and bought myself some appropriate church clothes.

For many years after that day, I served that "Jesus." The disappointed one that I could never please no matter how hard I tried. As a young pastor, I invested good money into my wardrobe. I had three nice suits, several shirts, a closet full of ties, and some kicking wing-tipped shoes in both black and brown! My wardrobe was never again going to disappoint Jesus, my master and lord.

No, that is not the Jesus I wanted to bring with me this time around. I wanted the real Jesus again. He was still there. He had never left me at all. He was still closer than a brother and He loved, accepted, and affirmed me just as Todd. No conditions or stipulations were attached.

And that, dear reader, is my deconstruction story. The story doesn't end there, however, and it shouldn't. Not for me or anyone else who is deconstructing. We must realize that deconstruction is a *means to an end,* and not the end itself. The reconstructing of our minds is about replacing outdated information with new and better information.

The dilemma in all of this is whether you and I choose to take the journey or stay planted in our limiting beliefs and unhappiness. Reconstruction, which is the main theme of this book, begins with one small step. I promise we will get there!

Reconstruction begins in our minds. Our minds are powerful. We each have unique ways of viewing the world. We refer to these as *perceptions.* In our next chapter, we will consider perceptions versus reality.

Chapter Two

THE PESKY PERCEPTION PROBLEM

"All that we see or seem is but a dream within a dream."

- EDGAR ALLAN POE

Philosophy and religion ask, "What is truth?" In this chapter we will attempt to answer science's question: "What is *reality*?" Reality may not be what you or I think it is. Reality can be many things to everyone, *Quot Homines, Tot Sententiae (many men, many opinions),* and that can be problematic. The root of the reality problem is *perception.* Perception is how we see what's in front of us. The problem or question with perception, according to Cognitive Research Science, is, *what if we are misinterpreting our perceptions? What if they are flawed or incomplete?*

Centuries ago, humans believed the world was flat. Why? Because it *looked* flat. Look to the left, look to the right...there is no round, it is all flat. That was common perception and it made perfect sense. However, Greek mathematician, Pythagoras, and Greek geographer Eratosthenes eventually proved empirically that Earth was indeed round. That is our current reality: a round earth.

Humans once believed that the Earth was the center of the entire universe. Why? Because it *seemed* that way and it made perfect sense. That was common perception. Polish astronomer, Nicolaus Copernicus, proved scientifically that we are not the center of the universe after all. We revolve around the sun. That is our current reality: Earth is not the center of the Universe.

What ties both examples together, is that new and better information was discovered, applied, and it eventually proven to update two new realities: Earth is round, not flat, and Earth is not the center of the universe. Though it looked that way, the perceptions were flawed and incomplete. To be sure, the new truth was hard to accept right away. In fact, early astronomer Galileo was condemned by the Catholic church in 1633 for believing and teaching that the Earth rotated around the sun. They had even put his discoveries on trial! Imagine discovering the cure for some disease, being arrested, and tried for blasphemy. Three hundred fifty-nine years later, on October 31, 1991, Pope John Paul II acknowledged publicly that the Roman Catholic Church had erred in condemning Galileo for asserting that the Earth revolves around the Sun. The Pontiff declared him forgiven.

Why are we so afraid to shift our perception when there is new and more accurate information available through proven scientific research?

I have four pets. There are two dogs, Toby, the Hyper-Beagle, and Lucy, the frumpy Rhodesian Ridgeback; there is a bunny, Mr. Snuggles, and a white dove named Angel, who is twenty-two years old. The dogs have free reign of the house (as well as of the humans!), but Mr. Snuggles lives in a 10' by 6' pen and Angel is in a cage. Angel's cage is small, but she never complains. For years, she has lived in this small cage with two perches and some toys. Every day, she sings, and it is a beautiful, soothing sound. She also laughs and barks like a dog... welcome to my world!

The cage is small, but she is completely content and happy. We sometimes open the door to her cage to see if she will fly out, but she never does. She is content to safely remain in that cage, even though we have plenty of room for her to fly around if she wished. Her cage is all she needs, all she has ever had, and all she will ever need, from her point of view.

Many Conservative American Evangelicals are stuck in the tiny cages of their limited beliefs. I know this because I was one of them for so long. The Bible was more than enough for me. If someone said that God had done something in their life that I could not confirm with scripture, I simply rejected it, and them. My spiritual beliefs were gathered over a thirty-year period. I worked hard to get and keep them. For a long time, no one could ask me theological questions or engage in discussion with me because I was unmovable in my conservative beliefs and perceptions. I lost friends and estranged loved ones because of my arrogance. I had my small, fundamentalist cage and everything I needed. I was not coming out of it. I was perfectly content and safe in there. I deconstructed all of that after discovering new and better information that altered my beliefs.

Conversely, Mr. Snuggles, the bunny, has no problem at all stepping out of his cage when we open the gate. He jumps around and around, looking for new things to explore (and power cords to chew). He isn't at all afraid to step out of his familiar environment and take in all that surrounds him.

In recent years, I have read books, attended seminars, webinars, and conferences to gather new and better information about faith, energy, and enlightenment. Slowly, I started venturing out of my conservative cage and exploring my own thoughts. I began to question the precepts which I had once held on to so tightly. I met with people from other world religions and even made a few friends. I attended churches from other cultures, denominations, and faith histories. A couple of them even had me come and speak. I was treated better by them than I ever was in any of my former churches!

I was shifting my perception and opening myself to new and better information.

Our perception of God, Jesus, Holy Spirit, Heaven, Hell, Homosexuality, Marriage, Divorce, and Morality is what it is because it has always looked that way and it made perfect sense. These insights have been passed down for generations and indoctrinated into believers everywhere. Church history is replete with people who challenged the popular beliefs of their day. Some were hanged, imprisoned, and exiled. For what? For shifting their faith perceptions based on new and more accurate information. Reformations and revivals happened as people began to see that God is much bigger than their mental cages will ever allow Him to be! They opened their mental cage doors and courageously ventured out. It changed the world! Let's take a quick trip down under.

The Australian Jewel Beetle is brown, dimpled, and glossy. Only the male can fly, and he does just that, looking for a mate. Female beetles are larger than the males, and don't fly. Mating occurs on the ground. The female beetle has a large, shiny brown body covered in dimples. A male flying in search of a mate will scan the ground below him, looking for a shiny brown object with a dimpled surface. And therein lies the problem.

The beetles almost went extinct some time ago. Males were flying and landing on a brown, dimpled, and glossy object of their affections and mating. The problem was that they were landing on brown, dimpled, glossy discarded bottles of beer in the outback. In order to preserve the Australian Jewel Beetle, Australia had to literally change the color of their beer bottles from brown to white to save this species. It is the quintessential story of men leaving women for the bottle!

The male only saw the gloss, the brown, and the dimples. It never occurred to him that he had mated with an inanimate object. Furthermore, the male risks being devoured by ants or drying up in the sun, still trying his hardest to please his false "partner." He was instinctively drawn to the familiar color and texture. Even while crawling all over the bottle, he could not discover his mistake. Likewise, our human instinct is to see what we want to see. To perceive what we wish to perceive, based on what we know and trust because it makes perfect sense to us. Is that so awful?

What if there is an alternative? Evolutionists postulate that we have natural intuitions to see only what we need to survive, rather than perceiving reality in its broader context. These evolutionary "hacks" exist to keep us safe and should be taken seriously.

"See that snake? Do not pick it up."
"See that cliff? Do not jump off it."
"See that hot oven? Do not touch it."

These are perceptual symbols that God created us with to keep us safe and alive.

The problem is that, like the jewel beetle and my dove, we like our reality as we perceive it. We don't like to admit we are wrong. But here's the point: Once we let go of our stubbornly intuitive but massively false assumptions about the God and the Universe, we open ourselves to new ways to perceive life's greatest mysteries. When we jettison our misinterpreted, incomplete, flawed perceptions and beliefs and choose to step outside the cages of our minds, we will begin to discover that reality is more fascinating and surprising than we've ever imagined.

This cognitive shift is the beginning of *reconstruction*. Reconstruction beckons us to surrender our long-held beliefs, mindsets, points of view, and opinions in favor of updated knowledge that leads to healthier attitudes and outcomes. Otherwise, like the Australian Jewel Beetle, we risk spiritual and mental extinction, or being devoured by the ants of our stubbornness.

This stubbornness we speak of is known as *Cognitive Rigidity*, which we will examine in our next chapter.

Chapter Three
THE COGNITION CONUNDRUM

"Cognitive psychology tells us that the unaided human mind is vulnerable to many fallacies and illusions because of its reliance on its memory for vivid anecdotes rather than systematic statistics."

— DR. STEVEN PINKER

"To know that we know what we know, and to know that we do not know what we do not know, that is true knowledge."

— NICOLAUS COPERNICUS

The scientific word for point-of-view is *cognition*. Your cognition takes many years to develop. It is the sum-total of all you have learned, everything you believe, and all your individual experiences. My cognition, or point-of-view could be completely opposite from yours regarding, well … anything. Therein lies the conundrum: *We are who and what we are, and we are unwilling to change. What we know is all we need to know.* Instead of remaining polarized by our differences, we should embrace and celebrate them!

During my tenure in local church ministry, I encountered various understandings about God, Jesus, the Holy Spirit, the Bible, Soteriology (the doctrine of salvation), worship, communion, tithing/giving, servanthood, evangelism, Protestants, Catholics, and the various expressions of these things. The conundrum is that everyone of us perceives these representations of faith in a myriad of ways. Thus, begs the inevitable question: *which expression is the correct one?* The answer is simple.

They all are ... according to our own unique perspectives .

As an evangelical pastor I held up the Bible as the final authority on all matters of life and principle. That viewpoint was indoctrinated to me in Bible college. I was warned of the potential dangers of doubting God and the Scriptures. *Sola scriptura—only the Bible.* All my sermons were centered around living up to the standards of God's word and the consequences for not doing so. I was a preacher of fear. Obey God, or else. Read your Bible every day, or else. Meditate on it day and night, or else. Bring it with you to church, or else. Leave it open during the sermon, or else. Stand in honor of its reading, or else. Memorize it, or else. Love it, or else. Hold it up against anything that dared to contradict it, even the Bible's own contradictions were our problem, not God's, or else! It's all part of the mystery. God's ways/thoughts are higher than our ways/thoughts. I believed that God superintended the copying of the inerrant original texts over thousands of years. *Sola-freaking-Scriptura!* God said it, that settled it, and I believed it! And by the way, you do too, got it? Anything less is heretical. B-I-B-L-E, that's the book for me. The end. *Ex cathedra.*

That was my expression of the Christian faith. There were other expressions more Jesus-centered. I merely dismissed them as the peddling of cheap grace. The social gospel was heresy to me. Catholics were all going to hell, along with all the people who reject, or have never even heard, the gospel. Collateral damage. Hell was hot and filling up more and more every day with unfortunate victims of pastors who didn't *preach the word* and their congregants who had the misfortune of being in their liberal, seeker-friendly churches. It was what it was—my cognition, or point-of-view of Christianity.

Would you like to know what turned my cognition around? It was, in fact, the *Bible*. John chapter one, verse fourteen, specifically. *The* WORD *became flesh and blood, and moved into the neighborhood*

(MSG, emphasis mine). That verse stopped me dead in my fundamental tracks.

The Word of God was the ultimate expression of God in his perfect and unique son, Jesus of Nazareth. The word was not a book, it was a man who is at once human and divine. Jesus is the Word of God. He is the fullness of every aspect of almighty God. I had been worshipping a book, not a man—not *the* man, the Lord Jesus. I would discover that the teachings and the ways of Jesus stood in stark contrast to much of what was known as *Adamic, Mosaic, Abrahamic, and Davidic*. Lots and lots of "ics," propagated by men like me. We were called Pastors and Scholars. The ancients were called Pharisees, Sadducees, and Rabbis. They upheld God's law as it was contained in the original manuscripts. They rejected Jesus and everything he represented as God in the flesh. Every good, kind, and noble thing Jesus did was harshly criticized by the religious elite. Sound familiar?

Meanwhile, people were being healed, delivered, and made whole by this man named Jesus. Twenty thousand people or more were fed by Jesus on a grassy knoll from a little boy's meager lunch, of which twelve baskets of food were leftover and everyone's bellies were full.[1] Jesus spoke of being sent to finish what God had started by doing His will on earth. God was with us, finishing what he started through Himself. John said that he *came unto his own (that's us), and his own rejected him (that's also us)*. Jesus made many bold proclamations about himself, as He was, *head and shoulders over other messengers from God*.[2] The other messengers were prophets, kings, scholars, and leaders like Moses or David.

What the heck was this guy's problem? Jesus was upending what people had believed for centuries with one simple, but not easy, commandment: *Love God, Love Others*.[3] What about the rest of the commandments? What about the sabbath? What about honoring your

---

[1] John 6:1-15

[2] John 3:31

[3] Matthew 22:35-40; Mark 12:28-34, and Luke 10:27a

father and mother? What about not bearing false witness? Who did this guy think he was?

Emmanuel—God with us. He breathed the same air we all breathe. He was fully human. He likely had bad breath in the morning. He farted, belched, peed, and pooped. He was warmed by the same sun as we are ... the one *He* created. He ate and slept. He was human like us but also contained all the divine essence of God within himself. He shared that divinity with the world and left us astonished.

Jesus challenged every cognition of every person everywhere. He created a holy conundrum that He brought with him from heaven to earth. He spent time with lowlife IRS agents, adulteresses, foreigners, lepers, the demonized, and the outcast. He restored life to a man who had been dead for four days. He restored our lives by giving up his own on a Roman cross. He pleaded for us to be forgiven while we mocked him as he hung on that same cross. He obliterated the cosmic separation we were told we had from God. He revealed that he has always loved us and always will. He supernaturally evacuated himself from a borrowed tomb, placing once and for all the seal of His majestic grace and forgiveness on our lives. Jesus left us with another part of himself, the Holy Spirit, so that we could do what he did and so much more. Through this he revealed that divine ability has always been inside of us.

What have *we* done? We have imposed our arrogance-blinded cognitions on the gospel narrative so that we can control the outcomes. We have murdered to spread this faulty expression of grace. We took what Jesus did and turned it into a religion that demands conformity and cooperation, held together by the Bible, which we have also hijacked for personal power and gain. We have become judges, prominent leaders, and modern-day Pharisees. We decide what is truth and what is not. We hold up our Bibles and pronounce the authority of scripture that we probably have not even read. We blindly follow along with the rest of the Bible thumpers and pick up their mantle of exclusion and mockery of the "least of us." We elected a President who is nothing like Jesus and held him up as the man, "God put in the White House."

Not me. Not anymore. My point of view has been altered due to deep deconstruction. In no way am I trying to imply that I am better than anyone. I'm still perfectly flawed me, but I see things much differently now. Unlearning thirty-plus years of personal theology was harder than I can say in words. It was like the death of a long-time friend whom you trusted and believed in for so long. I have experienced this type of loss both literally and spiritually. In some providential way, it was my dear friend Rick who planted the seed of deconstruction in my life. I brushed a lot of it off back then. When he died suddenly in 2013, I started reading the books he had recommended and began to understand his cognition. His death inspired me to write *The Renewing of Your Mind*, and I proudly dedicated it to him. The funny thing is that while I was deconstructing, I did not even realize that it was deconstruction, technically. I was amending my beliefs to be more like Jesus.

Not Jesus, the white-American-fundamentalist-evangelical savior. I had to free Jesus from my indoctrinated cognitions and just allow Him to be who He truly is. He is God who came to us and traded his perfection for our imperfection. He gave his own life to demonstrate how deep his love for us is and always has been.

I did not change right away. Before I discuss reconstruction, I want to caution you that deconstruction can lead to cynicism and a critical spirit. That was me for a little while. Be careful with that. Jesus loves all of us, even those who don't think as we do. The religious right, left, and middle are deeply loved and adored by Jesus, whose grace permits us to have our own personal cognitions, popular or not. I personally believe that our diversity, if united within the unmeasurable grace of God, could turn the world upside-down with love. I really believe this!

So, what have we learned so far?

We have learned that our perception isn't necessarily reality. Just because the earth looks flat doesn't mean that it is. Just because you perceive the Bible as the final authority doesn't make it so. Thus, breeds the cognition conundrum. Which of us is right? All of us. We are all on a journey. Our journey. I am not on your journey any more than you are on mine. When we come together with our various cognitions, or points of view, we create a larger, even better cognition. The conundrum transforms into a beautiful reality of living for each other rather than ourselves. I put you first, and you put me first. Imagine the possibilities!

Chapter Four
THE CASH COW CONFUSION

"No golden calf is needed for the relationship between God and God's people to take root in the world— only a community of willing individuals."

—C. ANDREW DOYLE

It has been said that we humans all have a "God-shaped" hole in our hearts, which is indicative of our deep need to have a god to worship in order to be whole spiritually and mentally. Everyone has their own image of God that is very personal to them. So much so that they are willing to fight for and defend it, even to the death. For centuries, humans have fought wars over religion. Their religion.

The late comedian George Carlin summed it up this way:
"Do you believe in God?"
"Yes."
"Do you believe in *my* god?"
"No."
(Points gun) *Kablam*!

In Exodus 32, Moses, the reluctant leader of the Israelites, who had rescued them from slavery, went up to the mountain to meet with the Hebrew God, whose name is, "I Am who I Am."[4] While Moses was away, the Israelites were feeling left out. They asked Moses'

---

4 Exodus 3:14

brother, Aaron, who had been left in charge, to make a god for them to worship.

The text doesn't indicate whether Aaron protested their idea. It seems that he was right on board with the request. Aaron asked everyone to give him all their gold jewelry. I have always wondered how people who had been enslaved for over four hundred years had gold jewelry. Was that standard Egyptian slave *accoutrement?* "Here, slave, wear these gold earrings while you build our pyramids ... "

I digress.

Aaron took their gold, melted it down, and fashioned it into a calf. Not a cat or a unicorn. Not a statue of some great ruler. Not a pair of praying hands. Not a bunny or a dog.

A calf. A golden one. Why?

The story of the golden calf, the greatest scandal of the wilderness period, is recalled in Deuteronomy 9:9-21, based on the fuller account in Exodus 32. Images of bulls and calves were common in Near Eastern religions. In Egypt, a bull, *Apis*, was sacred to the god Ptah and emblematic of him. In Canaanite literature, the chief god El is sometimes called a bull, although this may be no more than an epithet signifying strength, and the storm god Baal sires an ox in one myth. Did you notice that there were five gods in one paragraph? A lot of people and cultures have their own golden calves!

Why did all these people create all these gods for themselves?

You will recall from chapter two we discussed perception. Why did they worship these inanimate objects? Simple. They looked like gods. I mean, seriously, what does God really look like? Really? No one knows. Many have speculated. DaVinci, Michelangelo, Raphael, Salvador Dali, Jean-Francois Millet, and El Greco have all attempted to portray God through their famous paintings.

A few actors have portrayed God on film. George Burns, Morgan Freeman, Alanis Morrissette, and Octavia Spencer are among the most culturally relevant. Each one's portrayal of God is more tied to the characteristics of the actors, however. There are innumerable attempts throughout history to try and show how God is. Only one has ever succeeded ... Jesus.

Jesus of Nazareth was born in humble stature and died a humiliating death. In between those two events, he portrayed God in every way. Dr. Brad Jersak introduced us to *A More Christ-like God* in his book with the same title. The people were looking for a King; Jesus showed them a servant. They wanted a King who would cleanse the world of oppressors; Jesus washed their feet. Social outcasts were shunned and ignored; Jesus befriended and dined with them. The people wanted a condemning King; Jesus showed them forgiveness. Everyone's brazen imagery of God was annulled in the person of Jesus ... fully God, fully human. The real and authentic "golden calf" is actually a *lamb*.

The Israelites went wild in their "worshipping" of their golden calf. In return, they were forced by Moses to drink the powdered remains of their golden calf to punish them and then he had them all killed. The Law permitted him to do so. Killing people as an act of worship under the Mosaic Law was totally accepted but looked nothing like God.

To worship our lamb, however, is to help (not kill) the needy, feed the poor, and stand up for the oppressed. Not by raising up huge buildings and trying to abscond political power and influence. The Israelites choked down their powdered water leading to their death. Jesus told us that if we drink the water that he gives us, not only will it refresh us, but will spring up within us with eternal life.[5] He wasn't proclaiming this truth dressed in a silk suit. He was likely dressed in ragged clothing. He wasn't preaching at the First Christian Bapti-Presby-Costal Church, be assured of that.

Are you ready for this?

He was talking to a Samaritan woman at a well in the center of town. *A Samaritan woman.*

Whiskey. Tango. Alpha. Foxtrot.

Let me explain. In the culture Jesus was in, Samaritans were sworn enemies of the Jews (remember that Jesus was a Jew). Instead of rejecting the woman at the well and calling her a "dog" or a "half-breed,"

---

[5] John 4:14 (ESV)

like his Jewish contemporaries did, He offered her a refreshing drink, intimate personal conversation, and eternal life to an enemy of God's people who also happened to be a woman in a culture that was insanely male dominated.

What was the big deal about the Samaritans? Why were they so hated by the Jews?

The nation of Israel was divided into two nations in the days of Rehoboam (1 Kings 12). Israel was composed of the ten tribes to the north, and Judah was made up of Judah and Benjamin. The animosity between the Jews (inhabitants of the Judah, the southern kingdom) and Israelites began immediately after the division, as Samaria was the capital city of the northern kingdom (with Jeroboam as her first king). Rehoboam assembled an army to make war against Israel to reunite the kingdom, but God intervened through His prophet Shemiah (1 Kings 12:21-24). Later, in speaking of the reign of Abijam, Jeroboam's son, 1 Kings 15:6 says, "there was war between Rehoboam and Jeroboam all the days of his life."

Immediately after the division, Jeroboam changed the worship of the Israelites in 1 Kings 12:25-33. No longer did the inhabitants of the north travel to Jerusalem to offer sacrifice and worship (cf. Deuteronomy 12:5-14). Instead, Jeroboam set up idols in Dan and Bethel.

Later, after Israel's fall to the Assyrians, they began to intermarry with the Assyrians, contrary to Deuteronomy 7:3-5. Therefore, the Jews hated the Samaritans as "dogs," or "half-breeds."

It's true ... the ancient Hebrew culture had ugly disdain for dogs. To be identified as one of our furry little friends was the ultimate insult.

The Samaritans were also a continuous source of difficulty to the Jews who rebuilt Jerusalem after returning from Babylonian captivity (Ezra 4:10; Nehemiah 4:2).

Eventually, the religion of the Samaritans evolved to the point that they held only the Pentateuch (Genesis-Deuteronomy) as being the Law of God, rejecting all the books of poetry and prophecy. Furthermore, they claimed their copy of the Pentateuch was the only original copy (a claim still made today by what few Samaritans still survive). Obviously, this was/is a claim rejected by the Jews.

Jesus treated the Samaritan woman like a good friend. He didn't chase her from the well and tell her to get back over the wall to her own people. He showed her grace and offered her the highest blessing!

The propensity for men and women who say, "God is so good," or, "I am so blessed," almost always reflects financial or material blessings. When the job is lost, or the money stops flowing, is God still good? We need to separate money from grace. One has nothing to do with the other. Money by itself is not evil and is even nice to have but should never be traded as a replacement for authentic fellowship with Jesus.

The story of the Golden "Cash Cow" reminds us of this powerful truth—Jesus turns the deathly powdered water in our hearts into living water! There is no confusion there. Also, grace has no walls or boundaries. It is free and available to all! So, throw away your golden calves and take a great big gulp of the Living Water!

You will never thirst again.

Ever.

Chapter Five

REBEL WITHOUT APPLAUSE

"It is not rebellion itself which is noble but the demands it makes upon us."

– ALBERT CAMUS

Classic movies are one of my guilty pleasures. Hi, my name's Todd, and I am a hardcore cinephile. From silent movies of old to *Avengers: Endgame*, I have seen thousands of films. A few have stood out for me over the years, like *Rebel Without A Cause*, the movie that put James Dean on the map. After moving to a new town, troublemaking teen Jim Stark (Dean) is supposed to have a clean slate, although being the new kid in town brings its own problems. While searching for some stability, Stark (no known relation to Howard or Tony Stark) forms a bond with a mentally disturbed classmate, Plato (Sal Mineo), and falls for local girl named Judy (Natalie Wood). However, Judy is the girlfriend of neighborhood thug, Buzz (Corey Allen). When Buzz violently confronts Jim and challenges him to a drag race, the new kid's real troubles begin.

It deeply troubles me that the three stars of this movie, Dean, Mineo, and Wood, all died incredibly young. Some people are just not long for this world. They come into our lives, make a huge impact, and then they are suddenly gone forever at the apex of their careers. Jim Croce, Keith Green, Rich Mullins, Rachel Held Evans, and Rachel Joy Scott are notable untimely deaths from my generation. And let's not forget Robert Perry.

Robert Perry was not a famous man—at least not outside of the small community of West Mount, NC. He was the Sunday School Director at the church I had just began to serve as Minister of Music and Youth. Before I arrived, Robert was leading the choir and congregational singing. If anything was needed at the church, Robert was there to provide it.

I liked Robert right away. He was a funny fellow—always making people laugh. During the Sunday School hour, you could hear him yucking it up with someone in the hallways. Every Sunday he wore a Three Stooges tie. You could not be around Robert and not be smiling or laughing. In fact, he always kept a perpetual half-grin on his face underneath his puffy 1980s mustache. He was such a kind and helpful soul. He always told me, "Todd, you know I'll always do whatever I can to help you." And he meant it. The last time I saw him, that is exactly what he said to me with that genuine heart of his shining through the grin on his face. I loved him very much. All who knew him did.

Two days after Christmas in 1997, I received a phone call that Robert had died of a massive heart attack while playing basketball with his children, whom he adored. He was only 44. The heart attack was so massive that he was dead before he even hit the floor. This was my first time dealing with death as a minister. Death was something that happened to other people before that day.

Our pastor and his family were on vacation, and so as second in command, I immediately headed to the hospital to be with his wife and children. They took me straightaway to see him in the trauma room. As God is my witness, with a nasal-gastric tube in his nose and EKG wires everywhere, he had that same half-grin on his face! Even in death, he was a happy man. I have never forgotten that day or that man.

As a young minister and seminary student at that time, my focus was on doing *big things* for God. After all, William Carey said, "Attempt great things for God; expect great things from God." I had dreams of one day leading a large membership church, earning exceptional compensation, and creating even more big things for God!

I wanted to be a great man who did great big things for the kingdom of God. Dream big or go home, right? Wrong. So very wrong. The goals and plans I had in mind for greatness in ministry were way off the mark. The next Billy Graham … ? Come on, Todd.

Jesus had a different plan in mind for greatness. It was servanthood. Being a servant doesn't gain you recognition or huge salaries. It is seldom noticed by others. It is about making the world a better place by putting others above ourselves. Robert Perry never realized what a great man he was. If someone needed a ride, he drove them. If something was broken at the church, he fixed it. If someone was feeling sad, he cheered them right up! He never asked for anything from anyone in return. He was at his best when he was helping others.

Jesus did that. Robert Perry did that. They joyfully served others seeking nothing in return and made a huge difference in the world. Their world.

Robert died over twenty years ago, and yet I still think about him. That is impact. That is legacy. That is how to be great in the kingdom of God. Serve others, love others, and without reward. They will never forget you.

Jesus was a rebel without applause. He upset the religious elite each time they came to challenge him. He never went looking for arguments about the Law with the Pharisees, but they always came at him anyway. They never appreciated the grace-filled savior right before their arrogant eyes. We don't seem to appreciate him either.

He turned the world upside down, and yet we only give him two national holidays.

He gives us eternal life, and we give him one hour or two of our attention per week.

At least that was what I preached to people pre-deconstruction. Back then, that was the kind of preaching that would supposedly land you the big church. Our world encourages us to dream big and have big career goals. Ministers are not immune. Rebelling against that mindset is critical. It has all but destroyed the church-at-large. Numbers never, ever mattered. People always have.

Always.

What about you, friend? Do you want to make a big splash in the Kingdom of God? Do you want the accolades? The money? The prestige? I get that, I really do. Success like that has its rewards.

Jesus came to show us a better way—his way. Serve your world without the applause. My good friend and fellow author, Keith Giles was also a local church pastor for many years. When he left that behind, and went through deconstruction, he and his wife started a home church. Every dollar that was brought in went to help people in need. Neither Keith nor the church kept a penny for themselves. Today, he has authored a number of books and is a sought-after speaker. He would say that he doesn't do it for applause. He genuinely wants to help the world through his writing and teaching. He is also a mentor to many of us ex-pastors. I am thankful to know him.

We don't need or want applause when we are genuinely trying to magnify the great love of Jesus to the world.

And we never will.

Deconstruction strips us of all that pretentious piety and empties us of personal ambition or gain. At that point, we are poised to begin our journey of reconstruction.

Part Two
THE REFRAMING

Chapter Six

THE ROCKY ROAD OF RECONSTRUCTION

"Reconstruction goes hand in hand with reconciliation."

- NELSON MANDELA

Reconstruction isn't a new word in Christianity. It has been used for decades by the fundamentalist, reformed theonomic movement.[6] The movement included the works of reformists such as Rousas Rushdoony, Greg Bahnsen and Gary North;[7] it has had an important influence on the Christian Right in the United States, which is quite ironic if you think about it.

In keeping with the cultural mandate, reconstructionists advocate theonomy[8] and the restoration of certain biblical laws said to have continuing applicability. The movement declined in the 1990s and

---

6 Duncan, J. Ligon III (October 15, 1994). "Moses' Law for Modern Government." Annual National Meeting of the Social Science History Association. Atlanta, GA. Archived from the original on November 30, 2012

7 Smith, David L. (February 1, 2001). *A Handbook of Contemporary Theology: Tracing Trends and Discerning Directions in Today's Theological Landscape.* Baker Publishing Group. p. 214. ISBN 9781441206367.

8 Theonomy is a hypothetical Christian form of government in which society is ruled by divine law. Theonomists hold that divine law, including the judicial laws of the Old Testament, should be observed by modern societies.

THE RECONSTRUCTING OF YOUR MIND

was declared dead in 2008.[9] Christian reconstructionists are usually postmillennialists and followers of the presuppositional apologetics of Cornelius Van Til.[10]

One Christian denomination that advocates the view of Christian reconstructionism is the Reformed Presbyterian Church in the United States. Most Reformed Christians, however, disavow Christian reconstructionism and hold to classical covenant theology, the traditional Reformed view of the relationship between the Old Covenant and Christianity.[11] In contrast to where we are headed, *this* reconstruction deals with government, economics, and justice. These reconstructionists are practicing libertarians. They hold that murder, incest, adultery, lying about virginity, public blasphemy, kidnapping, and homosexuality are all punishable by death, as dictated by Scripture.[12] Capital punishment prescribed by the Bible has nothing to do with the type of reconstruction we will be dealing with, however. Our reconstruction is diametrically opposed to this type of mindset.

We identified the different types of deconstruction in the Preface. From here, we will build upon *faith reconstruction,* with the understanding that any of those listed in the Preface may apply directly to you, and that is okay. Everyone's reconstruction experience is unique to the individual. There is no reconstruction blueprint we all must follow. If there were, we would be right back where we started following

---

[9] Worthen, Molly (2008). "The Chalcedon Problem: Rousas John Rushdoony and the Origins of Christian Reconstructionism". *Church History.* 77 (2). doi:10.1017/S0009640708000590.

[10] Rosenberg, Paul (July 31, 2015). "Secrets of the extreme religious right: Inside the frightening world of Christian Reconstructionism". *Salon.* Retrieved March 2, 2019.

[11] Cunningham, Timothy R. (March 28, 2013). "How Firm a Foundation: An Exegetical and Historical Critique of the 'Ethical Perspective of [Christian] Reconstructionism'" Presented in *Theonomy in Christian Ethics.* Wipf and Stock Publishers. p. 7. ISBN 9781608994618.

[12] Durand, Greg Loren (October 31, 2014), *Judicial Warfare: Christian Reconstruction's Blueprints For Dominion,* Chapter 13, Toccoa, Ga.: Sola Fide Publishers, 2014, ISBN 978-0692240601.

religious rules created by man. Reconstruction begins by unhooking from religious thinking traps. These are also known as *Cognitive Distortions*. Here are some examples:

- **All-Or-Nothing Thinking:** In this religious mind trap, you either believe as everyone else does, or you are wrong. There is no room for meaningful discussions, questions, or opportunities to grow and evolve spiritually. This can also be called, *Black or White* thinking.

- **Theological-Reasoning Thinking:** You draw conclusions based on what you have been taught, rather than researching the information for yourself. For example, *God is wrathful and just, therefore when bad things happen, he/she caused it.*

- **"Should" Statements:** You are critical of yourself and/or others with "shoulds" or "shouldn'ts." "Musts," "Ought to's," and "Have to's" are similar offenders.

- **Labeling:** When someone doesn't believe exactly as you do, or if they question your beliefs, they can be labeled as, "backslidden," "liberals," "Bible thumpers," "holy rollers," or, "zealots." Labels create profound divisions within the faith community.

- **Overgeneralization:** "God said it, that settles it, and I believe it." The danger here is that the *overgeneralizer* is avoiding the task of thinking for themselves, researching information, and drawing their own conclusions.

Reconstruction begins with recognizing these cognitive distortions and discovering new and better ways of thinking. If you have thoroughly deconstructed, then theoretically all that remains are mental, emotional, and spiritual voids which are ready to be refilled with new and better information that serves your happiness and allows you to love and give freely. We are never more like Jesus than when we are giving and serving others. John 3:16 says, *For God so loved the world, He* gave. We should too!

There are many wonderful books that re-examine Christian "pillars," such as *Evangelism, Stewardship, Eschatology* (the second coming *of Jesus), Salvation, Prayer,* and many more. I will list these books in the Appendix section, and I encourage you to read them. These books have refreshed my soul in so many ways. Since there is already so much information like this available, I am going to sidestep those issues and defer to those who have skillfully addressed them for us.

In the next four chapters, we are going to plunge into deeper waters. There are parts of the Christian faith that Jesus laid out for us in the gospels quite plainly. Yet we continually avoid these things because it bids us to look deep within ourselves. Who wants to do that? It is so much easier to avoid those feelings and perhaps mask them with alcohol, drugs, or pornography. This was certainly the case with me.

Many of us have emotional baggage that would cause us to break down if we confronted them. I totally get that. With the help of my deconstruction, reconstruction, friends, medication, and a great therapist, I have been able to delve into my soul and root out things I had buried there for decades.

I believe we are created to feel. Why else would we have emotions? When we ignore our emotions and pretend the emotion is not there, it takes a toll on us, both mentally and physically. Recall my story from Chapter One. Not dealing with my depression led to addictive behavior and some physical issues as well. The mind cries out and the body suffers. Depression ensues. Hopelessness creeps in. Despair takes over. We feel drained. I am convinced that by surrendering to our emotions, we can find strength that we never knew we had.

The choice, of course, is yours, my friend. You can put this book down right now and keep on keeping on. However, I hope you will allow me the privilege of leading you down a rocky path—the rocky path of our feelings. If you are brave enough, you will experience a release and a refreshing you never thought possible. Jesus invites us to go deep. Many Christians today are literally drowning in the shallow end of their limited beliefs because they refuse to move. I don't want that for you, dear reader.

I need to give you a couple of disclaimers. First, I am not yet a licensed mental health professional. I am working on that. Second, you are unique, and you will have your own experience, though I cannot guarantee it will be easy for you. I make no such claims.

You are not alone on this journey, however. None of us are. If we look hard enough, we can find all the support we need. There are a lot of people who, like me, have deconstructed and then taken their first step on the rocky path to reconstruction. You will find their names on the list of books in the Appendix.

Take my hand, and let's walk this rocky road together. I will meet you in the next chapter!

Chapter Seven

LOVE, DEATH, AND RESURRECTION

"Listen carefully: Unless a grain of wheat is buried in the ground, dead to the world, it is never any more than a grain of wheat. But if it is buried, it sprouts and reproduces itself many times over. In the same way, anyone who holds on to life just as it is destroys that life. But if you let it go, reckless in your love, you'll have it forever, real and eternal."

— JESUS OF NAZARETH, JOHN 12:24-25 (MSG)

In *Star Trek 2: The Wrath of Khan*, Admiral Kirk said, *how we face death is at least as important as how we face life.* Later, he is confronted by his son, David, with the truth that until Spock died, he had never really faced death. *I cheated death*, he said, *and patted myself on my back for my ingenuity.*

Cheating death was never an option for Jesus.

Biologically speaking, the kernel, or wheat berry, is the seed from which a wheat plant grows. Contained within each kernel are acres and acres of wheat. Wheat is one of the world's most important food crops. It is believed that wild relatives of wheat first grew in the Middle East. Wheat was one of the first plants to be cultivated. It was grown about 11,000 years ago.[13]

Enormous changes in people's lives occurred because of wheat being grown. People began growing their own food and no longer

---

13   http://www.heirloom-organics.com/guide/va/guidetogrowingwheat.html

needed to wander in search of it. Permanent settlements were established because wheat provided people with a stable food supply. Soon people grew enough wheat to feed people from other lands. Once there was extra wheat available, trade between various cultures developed.

By 4,000 B.C. wheat farming had spread to Asia, Europe and North Africa.[14] New species of wheat developed because early farmers probably selected kernels from their best wheat plants to use as seeds for planting the following year's crop. That way, only the best wheat qualities were passed from one generation to the next. Soon wheat became an important worldwide crop.

Remember, all of this began when a kernel of wheat fell to the ground and died. The *only* way it can accomplish that massive worldwide growth is to die. In the world of wheat, death is necessary for life. In the world, life precedes death. In the Kingdom of God, death precedes life. Eternal life. The only life that really matters. Jesus of Nazareth demonstrated this principle for us on a Roman cross many years ago.

The cross is the center of human history. We mark our calendars by it. We make jewelry, tattoos, and steeples with the cross. For Christians, the cross is the centerpiece of their faith. It's the cornerstone of their belief system. It is a symbol. A symbol of what?

Death.

That's right. The cross is a place to go and die. Die is a verb. It is something you do—not something you wear around your neck or tattoo on your ankle. Jesus didn't go to the cross to cater to the paparazzi. There was no red-carpet event for him. Quite the opposite. The cross is the place where you go to die. Jesus knew what was coming.

As he prayed in the Garden of Gethsemane, he was under such stress and anguish that his capillary actions shifted. This is a medical phenomenon known as *hematidrosis*, where extreme emotional and physical stress causes the blood to form small clots that exit through the pores. He was literally sweating tiny clots or drops of blood.

---

[14] Ibid.

A mob appeared and Jesus was arrested. He was first taken before Herod. Herod didn't know what to do with him. Technically, Jesus had done nothing wrong. Herod then had Jesus taken before Caiaphas. Caiaphas was not in the proper jurisdiction, so he sent Jesus back to Herod. Again, Herod found no fault. The religious elite accused Jesus of telling people not to pay their taxes. Now Herod had something to work with.

I have learned over the years that when it comes to money, the local church will stand firm to protect their assets. You mess with the funds, and you have made an enemy. A formidable one.

Grace? No way.

Forgiveness? Not happening.

Mercy? Forget it.

Help? Get a job! God helps those who help themselves (this phrase is not in the Bible).

Jesus was falsely accused, by the way. None of the accusations were true at all. That didn't matter to the hostile crowd. If it even appears that you are interfering with the money, you're done. The people wanted him crucified. For political reasons most likely, Herod ordered that Jesus be flogged and then crucified. Roman soldiers took him away.

Flogging was a brutal punishment. If they followed standard Roman procedure, they would have tied him between two posts, hoisting him up where just the balls of his feet were touching the ground. This gave definition to the muscles. Romans were very skilled at this type of punishment. Keep in mind that Jesus had already been badly beaten before all of this happened.

The soldiers would then each grab a whip that had shards of glass, teeth, and stones woven into it. One soldier would start at the top, and the other would start at the bottom. In nearly perfect sync, they wrapped the whips around him and pulled with successive yanks that stripped the flesh right off his body. They took their time and did a very thorough job. His blood pressure dropped precipitously, and he was barely alive. The soldiers stopped the torture at just the right moment so he wouldn't die. His beard had been pulled from his face, and the Bible mentions that if you knew him before, you would not have recognized him after. His mother, his friends, and the religious leaders stood there and watched. There was nothing they could do to help Jesus.

Untied and forced to a standing position, he was then forced to carry the beam of his own cross uphill. As he did, the people who had praised him with *hosannas* less than one week prior, were punching and spitting at him while others hurled obscenities. His tongue was swollen from dehydration; he continued his long journey to the cross.

On the palm side of your hand there is a small indention between where your hand and wrist meet. Six to eight-inch spikes were driven into that spot on both hands, and then to his feet. The cross was lifted and dropped into a hole with such force that it separated his joints.

Hanging there, pinioned as he was to the cross, the fluids in his body began to fill inside of his midsection. He could inhale but not exhale. He was literally drowning. In fact, if you pierced his side, out would flow blood mixed with water. And there Jesus hung, suspended between eternity.

But they could not kill him![15] On the cross, he was the Captain, not the captured. His was the victor, not the victim. He was giving orders from the cross.

"Mother, behold your son."

"Son, behold your mother."

"Today, you will be with me in paradise."

"Father, forgive them, for they don't know what they are doing."

"It is finished."

"Father, into your hands I commit my spirit."

The mob didn't kill him. *He* decided when it was time for his spirit to depart, not them.

And then he died.

The *only thing* he stood to gain from all that physical torture and death was forgiveness for you and for me. John the Baptist once said,

---

[15] John 10:18

"Behold the Lamb of God, *who takes away the sins of the world.*"[16] How did he take them away? By dying.

Unless a kernel of wheat falls to the ground and dies, it will not bear any fruit.

On the third day, Jesus was vibrating at such a high energy level that death and the tomb could not keep him dead. The stone of his borrowed tomb rolled away, and he was no longer there. The fifteenth-century Easter hymn, *O filii et filiae,* refers to three women going to the tomb on Easter morning to anoint the body of Jesus. The original Latin version of the hymn identifies the women as Mary Magdalene, Mary of Joseph, and a woman named Salome. Matthew 28 only mentions Mary and Mary Magdalene. Regardless, they went to freshen Jesus' decaying body and quickly discovered he was no longer there!

The women ran back to the men and told them what they had seen (the first ever sharing of the good news was done by women!). The men then ran to the empty tomb to verify what the women had said. Peter the disciple peeked into the tomb and saw the Lord's clothes neatly folded. The men who followed Jesus for three years looked in the tomb and saw laundry. The women looked in and saw resurrection.

Death precedes resurrection in God's Kingdom.

By now you must be wondering, *what does all this have to do with me?* Fair question. The life, death, and resurrection of Jesus give us a blueprint of how we are to live now that sin has been eradicated. As I see it, following the risen Jesus gives us three types of lives to live interchangeably.

1. **Crucified Living:** Like the kernel of wheat, we must be willing to die to ourselves. Not a physical death. It is more of putting to death our selfish opinions, motives, and desires, so that we can freely express the pure, unadulterated love of Jesus to the world.

2. **Resurrected Living:** The resurrection of Jesus is not just an historical fact; it is also a lifestyle. He didn't overcome

---

[16] John 1:29

death on our behalf so we could say, "Way to go, God!" Remember that in the Kingdom of God, death precedes resurrection. It will never be any other way. When we die to ourselves, we magnify Jesus and put his perfect love on display to the world. Which brings to number three …

3. **Exchanged Living:** Jesus literally exchanged our humanity for his righteousness. He gave us what we could not give ourselves on the cross. Imagine the worst thing you've ever done. Recall the way it made you feel. Now take that bad feeling and multiply it by every human being who has ever lived, is alive now, and will live in the future. Then take all of that combined guilt and shame and put it into one man's heart. Jesus literally became unrighteous to make us righteous. He did this because he loves us, and for no other reason!

Romans 6:7 tells us that we are saved from sin and the consequences of sin. Period. There are no prayers to recite; there are no hands to shake; there are no cards to fill out. Jesus took care of everything for us. We are declared not guilty. The world calls us sinners. God calls us sons and daughters. You are as saved and free as you will ever need to be. Our choice now is to daily visit the cross, the empty grave, and to embrace the righteousness we have been freely given, and live our lives connecting to that divine energy we now live in.

You say, *Wait a minute! That is universalism!* No, it is truth. Jesus said, *it is finished (completed, done, ended, closed, mission accomplished).* He did not say, *it is* not quite *finished.* He does not need to go to the cross again. Romans 6 says that Jesus died *once for all.* Question: how many is *all?* Does the sum of *all* indicate that anyone is left out? Of course, it doesn't. All means all. Period. Jesus took care of it.

My son, Cody, has taught me more about God than anyone on Earth. Especially when he was just a small boy. In first and second grade, he seemed to be a magnet for bullies. There were specifically two boys giving him trouble. We spoke with his teacher and the problem seemed to stop for a short while. A noticeably short while.

I was picking him up and as he was getting in the car, I could tell he had tears in his eyes.

"What's wrong, son? Are you okay?"

"(The two boys) picked on me again."

"Where are they?"

"Over there."

I began to see red. I am generally a quiet, patient, and easygoing person. When someone hurts my children, however, Papa Bear comes out.

"Cody let's go talk to your teacher right now. I have had it with those two."

"No, Dad. I don't want to."

"Well let's go see those bullies and I will give them the what-for!"

"No, Dad. I don't want to do that either."

It seemed like my boy was cowering to these two creeps. I wanted to confront them.

"Cody, why don't you want to do anything to settle this? When we get home, I will teach you what my father taught me about bullies. If you hit them exactly right, you will break their noses. Then they will back off!"

I was livid. I was not going to let this go. My son was hurting, and I needed to fix it.

"I can't fight them, Dad. I just can't."

"Sure, you can. I will show you how! Why won't you let me?"

My son looked at me and said something that I will never forget as long as I live.

"Dad, if I hurt them, then I can't show them the love of Jesus."

My heart dropped into my stomach. The red went away. I was the pastor of a thriving church at the time, and yet my emotional default for bullying was revenge with extreme prejudice. Cody's default was Jesus. I was so ashamed. I apologized to Cody for my behavior and told him that we would pray for those boys every day. We did that. They eventually moved on to some other kid or stopped bullying. I hope it was the latter.

Die. It is the impulse of the selfless person. Denying yourself in favor of others is what Jesus modeled for us, and my son knew this at such a young age. I take no credit for that. Jesus made an impression on him, and it showed. He passed by revenge and went straight to forgiveness and compassion.

Following Jesus has nothing to do with saying the right words, memorizing Scripture, attending worship, giving money, witnessing to the lost, or shining your shoes. It is about freely giving love, compassion, and forgiveness to those who don't deserve it—no matter what it costs.

That is the place where miracles happen.

That is where people are healed!

That is where death becomes life!

That is resurrection living!

That is where reconstruction takes us if we are willing to go. Are you ready?

Chapter Eight
THE COLLAPSE OF COMMUNITY

"Alone, we can do so little; together, we can do so much."

—HELEN KELLER

As I write this chapter, I am quarantined at home with Laura and our pets while the COVID19/Coronavirus pandemic is in high gear. All over the world right now, people are safe in their homes and not able to go out without the possibility of spreading or catching this nasty virus. Churches have stopped meeting. Businesses have closed. The company I work for has deployed all of us to work from home. They sent us all the equipment we need to continue productivity. Nothing like this has ever happened in our lifetime. Quarantine has caused us to rethink our values as human beings and earthlings. Priorities have shifted.

One thing that this virus cannot destroy is our need for human connection. The miracle of modern technology has allowed us to have virtual meetings. Churches are having virtual services. People cannot physically go to church right now, so they are streaming the church services into their homes. Technology has literally changed the landscape of ministry. What is perfectly clear in all this chaos is that we really do need each other. Isolation has created a fresh yearning for things like hugs, handshakes, meeting a friend for coffee, going shopping, and visiting family.

The local church was once the center of its community. Life basically revolved around church activities. Co-workers invited each other out after work only to hear, "I can't tonight. I have church." Fellowship dinners were another staple of the faith community. I remember getting to know people better while sitting across the table from them. I began to develop what we call the "Preacher Gut." At local pastor gatherings, it was obvious I was not the only one. Sundays after church we would head to the all-you-can-eat steakhouse. It seemed that eating ourselves sick became the foundation of meaningful fellowship.

I began to realize that I had never preached or heard a sermon on gluttony, though the Bible does mention it unfavorably. I do recall the apostle Paul saying something about *buffeting* his body! If Paul hit the buffet, then it should be okay for me, right? Twenty pounds later, I realized that I needed to back away from the buffet. I started to politely decline dessert at dinners. Those poor church ladies looked at me like I had just stepped on their freshly waxed floor. They loved feeding us, and it really hurt their feelings when I passed on the heavy carbs. It's fun to look back on memories from church back then. Let's go back even further and examine the early church and reconstruct authentic, intimate community.

Acts 2:42-45 reads,

> "That day about three thousand took him at his word, were baptized and were signed up. They committed themselves to the teaching of the apostles, the life together, the common meal, and the prayers. Everyone around was in awe—all those wonders and signs done through the apostles! *And all the believers lived in a wonderful harmony, holding everything in common. They sold whatever they owned and pooled their resources so that each person's need was met.*"[17]

The book of Acts was written to chronicle the history of those first believers and their faith journey. *Their* faith journey ... not ours. We erroneously insert our own modern understanding of what church is into these verses. What we really need to do is take a quantum leap backwards in time and drop into their world to observe and understand their culture and point-of-view. Let's go!

---

[17] The Message. Emphasis mine.

KOINONIA 101

Our verse says that *all the believers lived in a wonderful harmony.* Notice the word *all.* In the previous chapter I asked the question *how much is* all? Can you really quantify *all?* Does all, in fact, literally mean *all?* We have no reason to doubt that every single believer, numbering around three thousand, were included in the *all* as well as the *wonderful harmony.* The word translated here in the Greek is *koinonia.*

Koinonia is commonly defined as *fellowship.* This fellowship is with God but more commonly with other believers. In the twenty-first century the word fellowship is associated with spending time with others. You can have a Sunday School fellowship, which is usually a potluck dinner (buffet!) in someone's home. There are usually games and lots of laughter.

Fellowship could be a night at the bowling alley. Laughter, conversation, maybe a beer and a hot dog, and even a little harmless competition can make a bowling fellowship one to remember.

Fellowship often refers to the church members. People are invited and encouraged to become a part of the *fellowship,* as if joining the church in membership indicates actual fellowship. Singing in the church choir was a slice of fellowship. In this case, it is more of a camaraderie between people working together to create beautiful music to add to the worship experience. Gathering in the sanctuary or worship center is a kind of fellowship. Families and friends congregate for a common experience of sitting, standing, singing, sitting, standing, praying, taking up the offering, hearing special music, a sermon, and the announcements.

For the record, I am in no way minimizing the value of these types of activities in church life. Some of my best memories involve being at church and participating. I have stood in front of hundreds of people over the years as a preacher and speaker. I treasure those moments with brothers and sisters in Christ. We didn't always know each other, but our belief in Jesus united us in a spirit of fellowship.

However, none of what I've just described is anywhere near authentic koinonia. Koinonia represents so much more than that. So much more than joint association, community, communion, joint participation, sharing your stuff, or contribution. To be sure, all those things fall under the umbrella of koinonia, but they still don't quite capture the actual meaning of the word.

Well, is there actually an English word that truly captures the original meaning of koinonia? It is a word one would never associate with fellowship in the church setting.

Intercourse.

Yes, my friend, you read that correctly. The closest word that captures the true essence of koinonia is intercourse. I am not referring to the physical act of having sexual intercourse. Sex is not the only type of intercourse one can have. There is a lesser acknowledged aspect of intercourse, and that is *intimacy*.

In the Old Testament, Jewish men had to be circumcised. A popular way to insult someone was to call them uncircumcised.[18] Men are still circumcised at birth today for health, not faith reasons. Some choose not to be circumcised. Why does it matter?

The Old Testament intention with circumcision was very spiritual. Boys are born with a hood of skin, called the foreskin, covering the head (also called the glans) of the penis. In circumcision, the foreskin is surgically removed, exposing the end of the penis. The spiritual trait of circumcision is related to intimacy. Sexually speaking, when a circumcised penis enters the vagina, there is pure skin to skin contact. The foreskin is not a barrier to the intimacy. Symbolically, this was the Hebrew way of demonstrating that there shouldn't be anything in our lives that hinders our intimacy with the divine.

Koinonia is another demonstration of intimacy between believers. No, we are not referring to orgies or any such thing. There should be no barriers between us and our fellow believers. That is intimacy. That is koinonia. What are some things that hinder intimacy among believers today?

- **Avoidance**: Think about how we engage each other in a typical church setting. We walk right past one another for the most part. Or we use shallow conversation. *How is your*

---

[18] See 1 Samuel 17:26

family? How is work? How is your health? Okay, see you next week! Avoiding each other leads to isolation which leads to loneliness which leads to depression which can lead to suicide in extreme cases.

- **Mental Health Issues**: There are instances where people have an actual physiological problem in their brain. This mental barrier can present as autism, Asperger's syndrome, or other types of neurological social disorders. There is no known single cause for autism spectrum disorder, but it is generally accepted that it is caused by abnormalities in brain structure or function. Brain scans show differences in the shape and structure of the brain in children with autism compared to in neurotypical children.[19]

- **Germaphobia**: Some individuals have genuine anxiety about touching others and catching sickness from them. You will see these precious people frequently washing their hands or using hand sanitizer. As I said earlier, there is a global virus that we are experiencing in real time. COVID19 is spread through human contact, so it is acceptable to have a little germaphobia when it is for unfortunate safety reasons due to pandemic.

- **Personal Privacy**: In the twenty first century, we have privacy fences, caller ID, texting, email, virtual chatting, social media, and tinted windows at home and on the car. All of these are tools used to avoid human contact. There are some who just prefer to keep to themselves and avoid human interaction outside of their immediate family and friends. When I was a boy, I knew all our neighbors. Today, I don't know my neighbors. I say hello in passing, but I don't even know their names. I am an introvert and an Enneagram 4. It is harder for me to make the first move. Harder, not impossible. I can't share the love of Jesus with others if I don't interact with them.

---

[19] http://www.autism-society.com

- **Culture**: Prejudice in some form has existed for centuries. In church growth meetings years ago, I was taught that people tend to flock toward those who are most like them. Dr. Tony Evans once said that Sunday morning at 11:00 am is the most segregated hour of the week. Serving on the mission field taught me a lot about prejudice. Mainly because I was on the receiving end of it. I was the person of color (or no color in my case). My mission partner and I had our lives threatened by locals in another country because of the color of our skin. I must admit that I wasn't prepared for that at all. Cultural differences can be a huge barrier to intimacy, be they from racial, religious, or financial status.

- **Emotionally Closed Off**: Continuing from number two above, there are people who either refuse or are unable to connect with their feelings. They put on their *mask* and pretend everything is good, so they don't have to feel their feelings. Feelings and emotions are a significant factor in intimacy.

- **Bitterness or Unforgiveness**: In *The Renewing of Your Mind*, I dedicated an entire chapter to the subject of forgiveness. When someone harbors ill will towards themselves, God, or others, it impedes intimacy or social connection. It is vital to your overall health to confront unforgiveness.

- **Politics and Religion**: We must learn to disagree agreeably, and to engage in meaningful dialogue as it pertains to one's political or religious views. Both topics are called *hot button issues* because there is so much passion beneath one's cognition. The easiest thing to do, it seems, is to just avoid those conversations. We need to do better here.

- **No Transformation**: When people see us in church on Sunday and cussing out the cashier at the grocery store on Monday, they become disillusioned. If Jesus can't change your life, how can he change mine? Renewing and reconstructing our minds creates transformation from the inside out. Transformation opens many doors to koinonia and intimacy.

- **Lack of Understanding**: Some people have a diluted understanding of what true, authentic intimacy looks like. This misunderstanding can begin in childhood. If your parents are closed off and don't show their feelings, you can become closed off as well. If one is sexually abused at a young age, it hardens the sections of the brain that trigger healthy emotions. That is why I have spent so much time on this chapter. I desire to know what intimacy is because I want it in my life. My word for 2019 was *authenticity*. My 2020 word is *intimacy*.

After leaving the ministry, I stopped attending church anywhere for a long time. A couple of sporadic visits to local churches only reinforced my desire to stay away from it. One day in late 2019, I received a LinkedIn message from a pastor I was friends with but had lost touch. This message got my attention in a couple of ways. First, I rarely check my LinkedIn page especially for the message feature. Second, Kevin and I were not *close* friends. We were acquainted through one of my former coworkers and my curiosity about his campus ministry at the University of South Carolina. We lost touch, and that was that. To hear from Kevin out of the clear blue made me consider that this may have been providential.

We met for coffee one day and I shared how I left the ministry, the church, my beliefs, and my faith behind. We talked about deconstruction. He understood. He listened. He got me. We really connected in that Starbuck's that day. I couldn't remember the last time I had that deep of a connection with someone, especially another pastor. During this time, I had also just finished reading *Searching for Sunday*, by Rachel Held Evans. That book helped me learn to love the body of Christ again.

Laura and I decided to visit his church, Kinetic Church,[20] one Sunday. I felt ready. It was a small group of people in a big auditorium at one of the local colleges. The worship leader/associate pastor sang horribly off key. Kevin's message was not flashy, but it had substance

---

20 http://www.kineticchurchsc.com

and I took a lot of notes, which I seldom do. I loved it! I had discovered authenticity in a local church of all places. I loved that the singer was off key! He was real. He wasn't putting on a show, He was making a *joyful noise*. I couldn't believe how moved I was by the service.

After church, Kevin invited us to take part in their Life Group, held at his parents, Sam, and Becky's home. We attended the group every week for several weeks. It was intimate. People were able to share their struggles openly in a safe place.

One night, Laura and I attended Life Group with heavy hearts and minds. We had some serious financial troubles and were facing eviction. We had no money and no solution. I shared this with the group, and something wonderful happened. As I shared my sad story, I noticed that everyone in the group was listening intently. The look on their faces indicated that they were empathetic to our struggle. They were in it with us. I don't like to share my stuff and be vulnerable like that, but I was so glad I did.

Early the next morning, after a sleepless night, I got a text message from Kevin, stating that he had been awake most of the night thinking about and praying for us. Kevin is an extremely generous and giving man. I know if he had a wad of cash on him, he would have gladly given it to us. That's not the best part of that story.

Kevin and our life group had joined Laura and I in our problem and sat there with us. We were not alone in our struggle. We had their love and support without judgment. Our problem was their problem. It was koinonia. I had never experienced it that profoundly before. I no longer cared if we were evicted or not. We had koinonia with a group of believers. It was magical. Our money problem was solved that very day in a completely unexpected way. For the first time in a long time, I felt connected with God and fellow believers. Deeply connected. I want that for you too, my friend. More than you can imagine.

The early believers in Acts showed us what koinonia looked like. They ate together. They shared their stuff with everyone else. Most importantly, there was intimate intercourse. Connection. Intimacy. Koinonia.

They had it then, and we can have it now. First, we must deconstruct our current mindset about community, and then reconstruct it with true, authentic, and intimate understanding of koinonia. My friend, if you can catch hold of this wonderful harmony, you will never be the same. As more of us realize true koinonia, the terrain of church will never be the same. If we can spread koinonia with the same fury as the COVID19 virus or common cold, the world will never be the same.

I never want to be the same again. I have had decades of the same old, same old. I'm so tired of it. Christianity from a distance no longer appeals to me. I'm ready for more koinonia!

Aren't you?

Chapter Nine
THE FALLACIOUS FEAR FACTOR

"Fear has a large shadow, but he himself is small."
—RUTH GENDLER

"Fear is an incompetent teacher."
—ADMIRAL JEAN-LUC PICARD

Most of us are afraid of something. I have a crippling fear of heights. I think my fear is more of *falling* from great heights than the height itself. I have no idea when or why this fear manifested. Another fear of mine is *losing control*. I have a neurotic need to be in control of my faculties and surroundings. It's regulated now ... mostly.

Have you ever stopped to think about why you fear certain people, places, or things? Is it such a bad thing to fear? As I mentioned in Chapter Two, we have built-in evolutionary tools in our brains to help us survive. Fear is one of the tools that keep us from harming ourselves. If used properly, fear *can* be a good thing to have. In this chapter, we will explore the concept of fear and its many contexts.

Fear has gotten a bad rap, and it's not as complicated as we try to make it. A simple and useful definition of fear is: *An anxious feeling, caused by our anticipation of some imagined event or experience.* Fear, like all other emotions, is basically information. It offers us knowledge and understanding—if we choose to accept and embrace it sensibly.

There are many meanings of fear depending on the context. Many books, podcasts, and blogs are out there that delve into the basic fears that we all have. Dr. Karl Albrecht lists five fears of which almost all of our other so-called fears are manufactured. These are:

1. **Extinction**: The fear of annihilation, of ceasing to exist. This is a more fundamental way to express it than just "fear of death." The idea of no longer being arouses a primary existential anxiety in all normal humans. Consider that panicky feeling you get when you look over the edge of a high building.

2. **Mutilation**: The fear of losing any part of our precious bodily structure; the thought of having our body's boundaries invaded, or of losing the integrity of any organ, body part, or natural function. Anxiety about animals, such as bugs, spiders, snakes, and other creepy things arises from fear of mutilation.

3. **Loss of Autonomy**: The fear of being immobilized, paralyzed, restricted, enveloped, overwhelmed, entrapped, imprisoned, smothered, or otherwise controlled by circumstances beyond our control. In physical form, it's commonly known as claustrophobia, but it also extends to our social interactions and relationships. This is a big one for me. I like to be in control of my life and body.

4. **Separation**: The fear of abandonment, rejection, and loss of connectedness; of becoming a non-person—not wanted, respected, or valued by anyone else. The "silent treatment," when imposed by a group, can have a devastating effect on its target.

5. **Ego-Death**: The fear of humiliation, shame, or any other mechanism of profound self-disapproval that threatens the loss of integrity of the self; the fear of the shattering or

disintegration of one's constructed sense of lovability, capability, and worthiness.[21]

As we continue this chapter, we will explore fear in the context of faith in God. The Bible has many verses that use the word fear. In carefully studying the Bible, however, we realize that there are basically two kinds of fear in the context of faith.

1. Fear of God
2. Fear of Punishment

For the remainder of this chapter, we will look at two popular but often misunderstood verses that include one of the two fears above. As we reconstruct our faith, I believe it is essential to spend some time with authentic fear and understand how it can work against us as we seek to evolve and grow spiritually through reconstruction.

ECCLESIASTES 12:13

"When all has been heard, the conclusion of the matter is this: Fear God and keep His commandments, because this is the whole duty of man."

In this verse, the word *fear* is translated from the Hebrew word, *yare'*. The word refers to a reverence, awe, drawing near to, astonished by, respect for, or an inspiring object. The book of Ecclesiastes is written to instruct a younger crowd about what is profoundly important in life. It is not a sermon meant to belittle. It's an expression of joy from one who has experienced it for himself!

The fear of God here includes all the graces of the Spirit, and the exercise of them; reverence of God, love to him, faith in him, and in his Son Jesus Christ; hope of eternal life from him. The actual author of Ecclesiastes is unknown, but the superscription in Chapter 1:1 attributes the book to *Qohelet* (commonly translated *preacher*, Greek

---

[21] Albrecht, Karl. *Practical Intelligence: the Art and Science of Common Sense.* New York: Wiley, 2007.

ekklēsiastēs), who is identified as *the son of David, king in Jerusalem*, words commonly reserved for King Solomon. However, I believe this is a prophetic reference to Jesus.

One of my clients told me about her childhood memories of her stepfather. In her words, he was *just horrible*. When I asked her why, she responded, *when he first came into our lives, he was kind and gentle. He was a pastor, and he seemed to really love us. His wife had left him, and they had no children together. He embraced her and her brother and sister as his very own. Things were great for a while. Because of his divorce, he was forced out of the ministry. After that, he became angry and bitter. We were an annoyance to him. At times it seemed like he was just watching and waiting for us to do something bad so he could yell at us. He started drinking heavily, and to be honest, we were all afraid of him.*[22]

As believers, many of us come from similar childhoods. As a result, many of us saw God as a mean stepfather just waiting for us to mess up so he could punish or smite us. Sadly, many preachers have portrayed God this same way through the centuries. They teach that abused women should suck it up and honor their husbands by staying and taking their lumps to glorify God. They declare without apology that any natural disaster is God's way of punishing the world. They portray God as a merciless taskmaster, who has a plan for our lives—to somehow use us in obedience to his will—but against our own will, and we must fear him.

The Preacher in Ecclesiastes paints a vastly different picture. Here we see that God is one to be revered and enjoyed. God looks and acts just like Jesus. Jesus was not wrathful and vengeful. He was not lurking to see who would screw up next. He didn't walk around with a yardstick to smack the knuckles of those who just couldn't measure up like an old schoolmarm.

Jesus said, *The Father and I are one.*[23] *Whoever has seen me has seen the Father. How can you say, 'Show us the Father'? Do you not believe that*

---

[22] Story used with permission.

[23] John 10:30

I am in the Father and the Father is in me? The words that I say to you I do not speak on my own authority, but the Father who dwells in me does his works. Believe me that I am in the Father and the Father is in me.[24]

Notice Jesus never described himself as wrathful and a murderer of his own creation. God is not that way either. I know what you are thinking, *Well, what about all those Old Testament stories that clearly display God as wrathful?* I'm glad you asked.

Part of reconstruction is learning to see the Bible as literature. It is filled with stories, poetry, history, and prophecy. For centuries, the Hebrews were taught and believed that one day God was going to settle business with all their enemies … much like the way Michael Corleone took out the heads of the five families in *The Godfather.* Even those who walked with Jesus while he was on earth were waiting for him to take vengeance on their enemies and establish a government where he is in charge and protects only God's chosen.

Much of the Old Testament is written about war. Sometimes God's people won and sometimes they didn't. Prophets like Isaiah wrote about the coming *day of the Lord,* when he would come in power and slay everyone who gets in his way. Most of us have heard the words, "Just wait till your father gets home!" This was the mindset of the ancients as they waited for God the Father to come home to earth and punish the evil doers with his cosmic belt. According to tradition, the prophets maintained a position on the wall of the temple, from where they would receive a word from the Lord for his people. Then they would tell a *herald,* who would take that word to the people preamble by a, *thus saith the Lord.*

I spent some time in the Charismatic/Third Wave movement about twenty years ago. I was introduced to speaking in tongues, giving someone a word of knowledge, and praying over people as they dropped to the floor. I attended monthly pastor's meetings with the charismatic pastors from all over the city. I met some amazing people there. At every meeting someone would come to me afterward and tell me that *God has given me a word for you!* It was usually along the

---

[24] John 14:9-11

lines of my church growing, my ministry expanding, or that God was about to unleash financial blessings on me. In time, I was doing the same thing in my Southern Baptist church, to the shock of my congregation. This was my very first pastorate. Those precious people loved me right through my charismatic phase. A lesser group would have run me out of town with pitchforks!

My point is that there were so many *words from God* to me and from me that it was becoming ridiculous. Prophecy was basically reassuring people with what they wanted to hear. I was good at reading people and was almost always right on the money. Almost. Years ago, someone said that fellow Wisconsin native and psychic, Jeane Dixon, *must be from God. She's correct 90% of the time!* I prefer to think that 100% correctness would better qualify her for that notoriety.

The ancient prophets possibly operated in the same manner. *You want war? God says it is coming! He is going to smite all his enemies! Afterwards, he will prosper his chosen people. You will find your true love. You will come into a lot of wealth.* If we take these prophesies literally, we place ourselves in a precarious position. We use our words to instill fear in others.

The second part of the verse uses the phrase, *and keep His commandments, because this is the whole duty of man.* If we are afraid of God, words like *keep* or *obey* seem to conclude with an unwritten *or else!* Jesus gave us this commandment, *Love God, love others.* He called this the greatest commandment of all. The word *duty* is not even found in the Hebrew text. It was added later. The Hebrew literally reads *this is the whole of man.* Following Jesus is not about obedience and duty. By loving God and loving others, we become whole and peaceful.

We never have to be afraid of God, for any reason, at any time whatsoever! Want to see what God is like? Look at Jesus. As a matter of fact, the Bible tells us to have *no fear* 365 times. One reminder for every day of the calendar year! If fear is the driving force of your faith, I encourage you to take a closer look at that and revisit the source those beliefs. Fear creates panic, stress, anxiety, high blood pressure, depression, agoraphobia (fear of leaving your house), and covers your life with stifling uncertainty.

On the cross, Jesus absorbed our worst fears and anxieties. We no longer need to live afraid! Isaiah 43:1 says, *Do not fear, for I have redeemed you; I have called you by name; you are Mine.* God beckons us not to fear or worry. Fear and worry decrease our hope and limit our victories. Let's examine our second text on that note.

2 TIMOTHY 1:7

"For God has not given us a spirit of fear, but of power and of love and of a sound mind."

This verse indicates that fear is a *spirit* that does not come from God. This spirit is a normal, natural flight response to a danger in our surroundings. ... It intends to keep you from fulfilling the destiny that God has on your life; from living a joyful, spirit led existence where you give to others out of the overflow of love in your own life. The Greek word translated fear is *deilia,* meaning *cowardice.* Picture the cowardly lion in *The Wizard of Oz.* He was nervous, anxious, and the smallest thing would cause him to explode with fear. Also, recall Cadet Hooks in the movie, *Police Academy.* You will not see a better (or more humorous) portrayal of cowardice and timidity.

This cowardice or timidity that *deilia* describes is not from God. This type of fear originates in our minds. My wife Laura loves to watch crime drama on television. Sometimes the perpetrator steps out of a shadow and grabs the victim's mouth so they can't scream. He then ties them up with duct tape and throws them in the back of his van or in his trunk. Because of this visual exposure, she is extremely cautious when she is out by herself. She parks under a well-lit area as close to the store as she can get. Why? So that no one can jump out of a van and kidnap her! She is afraid because of the images she has seen on television. Fear causes these images to be stored in our subconscious mind. But there's more ...

Fear is one of the most visceral emotional reactions you can have, so there must be a clear reaction in the brain when you get scared. Fear originates in a tiny part of the brain called the *amygdala*. One of the amygdala's functions is to connect emotions with memories. A study at Cambridge University looked at the brains of ten people who were afraid of spiders—and we're not talking mild heebie-jeebies, but certifiable DSM-diagnosed arachnophobia. A spider is probably the absolute worst thing they could see while lying in a dark brain scanner. Can you guess what the researchers did next? That's right, they showed them spiders while lying in a dark brain scanner.[25] Unsurprisingly, their brains reacted, and were compared to the brains of people who were not afraid of spiders. The reactions appeared as a tiny black dot—the amygdala. The picture on the brain scan is insightful. On the fearful brain scans, the amygdala is a tiny speck surrounded by the open space of the brain. It makes you think that fear is not as bad as we think.

Those who were not afraid of spiders had no reaction in the amygdala. You could be one of those fearless few. Remember that fear can be a good thing. Those without fear can run the risk of serious injury or other kinds of trouble. I once had a neighbor who was without fear. In the time that I knew him, he had been stabbed, shot, and is now in prison. Fear may have actually helped him change the course of his journey.

The bottom line is this: *Don't fear* fear! Instead, use the brain that God gave you to increase your knowledge and understanding of the divine source so that you can exhibit power, love, and a sound mind. James 1:8 points out that not having a sound mind causes mental instability.

You have deconstructed your faith system. You are now trying to rebuild or reconstruct your faith by obtaining better, updated information. I want you to know, once and for all, that God is not mad at

---

[25] https://www.cambridgebrainsciences.com/more/articles/what-fear-looks-like-in-the-brain

you. He does not hate you. He is not disappointed in you. He is not going to destroy you or toss you into a lake of fire.

Reconstruct your faith on this sure foundation: as far as you and God are concerned, you have nothing or no one to be afraid of. God is love ... and He loves *you!*

In our next chapter, we will build upon those three beautiful words, *God is love.*

Chapter Ten
THE POWER OF PRESENCE

"Walk together. Feel the heart beats. Experience the presence. This is how to be thankful."

- AMIT RAY

One of my personal heroes, the late Jim Rohn, once said, "wherever you are, *be* there." I always found that quote rather curious. Where else would I be? With Mr. Rohn, however, it is never quite that simple. The last time Laura and I went out for dinner, I was amazed at the number of people at their tables with their cell phones in hand, effectively ignoring one another. Then I looked at my own hand. Oops ... cell phone. Laura, too. I finally understood the quote. Mr. Rohn was talking about being *present*.

Several years ago, my children, Cody, Jenna, and Katie, each wanted to try out a sport. Jenna picked soccer, Cody picked tee-ball, and Katie picked softball. It was a busy time getting everyone where they needed to be each week, but I really enjoyed going to their games. None of my brood were star athletes, but they tried hard and learned from the experience. The parents at these games were all very pleasant and cheered for both teams. Most of them, that is. The other parents were completely tuned out. They were talking on cell phones, working on their laptops, reading, or chatting with other parents at the concession stand. Clearly, they were not present in the moment. They were missing it. People can spend all kinds of money on tickets to movies, sports events, ballet, and concerts. What's the point of spending that money if you are not going to at least try to be there? I don't mean show up. I mean *be there*.

I mentioned earlier that the world in which I am writing is under quarantine and practicing social and physical distancing. The few who do venture out wear protective masks and gloves while maintaining a six-foot distance from one another. Never has the need for human contact been so obvious. The COVID19 virus is teaching us the importance of being there for and with each other. Humanity for once is on equal footing. Racial, political, financial, geographic, or social status doesn't create immunity to the danger. We are discovering and rediscovering the joy of being connected as human beings as well as how vulnerable we all are. Simple things like going out to dinner, getting coffee with a friend, going to the mall, bowling, sport events, going to church, visiting loved ones, or having people over have suddenly been taken from us in order to protect us from the virus.

I am a textbook introvert. I used to pride myself on how much I enjoyed just staying home rather than being social. How I wish I had said yes to more invitations to be with family and friends. I can't even converse with my neighbors without maintaining the six-foot difference. Summer will be here soon. There could be a ban on swimming or fourth of July barbecues. We may not be able to go to the beach at all. We humans have really noticed how much we take these things for granted. Another thing we have seen increase during this crisis … people helping people, showing up for each other, and just being there. It reminds me of a story Jesus told in the parable of the Good Samaritan.[26]

In chapter four, I showed you why the Jews in Jesus' day had such disdain for Samaritans. This was a deep social rift. For a Jew to even look at a Samaritan would cause him to have to tear his garments in repentance for blasphemy. In the 21st Century, we still have more than our share of racial and social divides. Our problems pale in comparison to the utter hatred and spite the Jews felt for the Samaritans. So, who came up with the idea of a *good* Samaritan?

[26] Luke 10:25-37

When I was a boy, I spent nearly every weekend during the year with my maternal grandparents. Much of who I am today is owed to their influence. They taught me some wonderful lessons. Some of the lessons were hard. One Saturday afternoon, my Grandma pulled me away from cartoons and said, *I want you to be a Good Samaritan.* I had no idea what she meant. Across the street was an elderly gentleman mowing his lawn. Grandma told me to walk over and mow it for him. I was less than excited about the idea, but I could never say no to Grandma. I walked across the street and tapped the man on the shoulder.

"I'm here to mow your lawn for you, sir. My Grandma sent me over."

He said, "How much money do you want?"

I told him I would mow it for free. He accepted my offer. He was obviously fatigued and happy to have the relief. It only took me about forty minutes to complete the job. I was satisfied with my work. Honestly, are there many things more rewarding than viewing completed yard work? The kind elderly couple invited me to sit on their porch and have some lemonade with them. It was a perfect southern moment, and they treated me like I was a hero. I didn't get it. I just mowed a lawn. Seeing the look on their faces, however, made me glad I got to be a Good Samaritan. The Bible paints quite a different picture of what the Good Samaritan really was.

WHO IS MY NEIGHBOR?

A man approached Jesus on day. He was a lawyer—someone who obviously knew the law very well. He smugly tried to trip Jesus up with a question. *Teacher (not Lord), what must I do to inherit eternal life?* Jesus knew what the lawyer was doing and threw the question back at him. *What does the Law say?* There was no doubt that he knew the answer. *You shall love the Lord your God with all your heart and with all your soul and with all your strength and with all your mind and love your* neighbor *as yourself.* Jesus told him that he was right and to do that and live.

That was too easy.

The lawyer had one more question to try and befuddle Jesus. The answer to this question could possibly have gotten Jesus arrested. Behind this question was centuries of prejudice and hatred we cannot even begin to comprehend. I imagine the lawyer's face having a smug grin with a "gotcha" look in his eyes. Here was his question:

And who is my neighbor?

The question, and the way it was asked, indicates that the lawyer wouldn't be thrilled with any answer Jesus would give him. Jesus had two choices: say nothing or say the wrong thing. The Son of God gave himself a third choice. He told a *parable*, or an earthly story with a heavenly meaning. It is the story of a traveler walking from Jerusalem to Jericho. This particular road was well known for being a hotspot for robbers and thugs.

The man was jumped by a couple of these bad guys, beaten, stripped, and left for dead. While he lay half dead beside the road, a priest happened by. Jesus said he simply moved to the other side of the road, ignoring the wounded traveler, and going on his journey.

Have you ever passed by the scene of an accident or crime scene because you don't want to get involved? Of course you have; we all have at some point. We have places to go, and surely someone else will come along and help the poor victims. They say, *our taxes pay their salaries, right?* Whatever his reasons may have been, the priest walked right by him.

Next, a Levite happened upon the ailing traveler. Levites were higher in rank than priests. They had important responsibilities in the Temple. If anyone would stop and help, surely it would be the Levite ... or not. He also passed by on the other side of the road. He probably had a Levite meeting to get to. Maybe it was a budget team or *Priest Search Committee* meeting. Maybe he had to pick the Sunday music set or control the fog machine. Whatever the reason, it was more important than helping a suffering traveler.

The third and final contestant was ... wait for it ... a *Samaritan*. Undeniably, the lawyer's face turned from smug to *What the ... ?* The Samaritan went right to the injured sojourner—he didn't pass by on the other side like his predecessors. Next, the text says that the Samaritan *saw* him. The Greek word, *idon,* connotes looking at someone intently, closely, and not passively. The Samaritan took detailed notice of the man's injuries. The word used earlier for *beaten* is where we get our English word *trauma.* The man was clearly traumatized. We will look at trauma a little later.

The Samaritan also had compassion on him, according to the text. The word for compassion is not just a feeling sorry for someone. It is a compassion that affects you so viscerally that you must act. That's what I like to call *Jesus Level Compassion.* That level of compassion compelled Jesus to the cross.

As we continue examining this classic parable, I'd like to show you three qualities that translate into a genuine neighbor like the Samaritan.

A GENUINE NEIGHBOR GIVES OF THEIR TEMPORAL RESOURCES

Time is a non-renewable commodity. You spend it, it's gone, and you can't ever earn it back. Time is more valuable than money. Ponder that statement for a moment. You can never earn more time, nor can you buy it. The phenomenal philanthropist Andrew Carnegie desperately wanted more life. He felt he could make a lasting contribution to society if he had ten or twenty more years. He offered two-hundred million dollars for another decade or two. But no one could accommodate him. Why? Time is more valuable than money, and it cannot be bought. The Samaritan interrupted his journey to help the man. He sacrificed time that he would never get back. He did this for a stranger.

According to Nielson, we watch thirty-four hours of television per week. The average work week is forty hours. Mashable.com says that we spend 6.9 hours a week on Facebook. It's over eleven hours if we have a smart phone or mobile device. Barna Christian Research determined that believers spend fifty-two minutes per week reading the Bible. Basically, we spend more time in the shower than we do reading our Bibles, which sounds legalistic, but I was just intrigued by the numbers.

Did you make time for a stranger this week? Did you introduce yourself to a neighbor? Did you personally welcome someone new at work? Did you withhold a smile that may very well have changed the course of someone's life? An investment of our temporal resources, or time, is an investment that will never yield a bad return.

People around us have been beaten physically, emotionally, financially, and spiritually. Most of us have the time to help them. If we don't have it, we can find it. Time is more valuable than money. Loneliness can also be traumatizing. Just spending time with someone can change their lives. At least we can make their day brighter. Many elderly people are in nursing facilities, and many are there alone. Human interaction brightens their day more than if you gave them a million dollars. Try it!

A deacon in one of my earlier churches was very faithful in visiting the shut-ins on his list. One memorable lady was Mrs. Lucille. Mrs. Lucille was a widow and lived alone. She had a son who was a pastor and he lived upstate, about two hours away. He came to visit when he could. Other than her caregivers, Jim was the only person to regularly show up for her every single week. Every Sunday after church he stopped by. He often brought his family and Mrs. Lucille was so happy to spend that time with them. Whenever I visited her, she would say anything to get me to stay longer. All she needed from me was time. We each have one hundred and sixty-eight hours per week. If we work forty or fifty hours a week, that leaves us one hundred and eighteen hours! If we can't find time for others who need it, perhaps we seriously need to learn time management.

A GENUINE NEIGHBOR GIVES OF THEIR PHYSICAL RESOURCES

What did the Samaritan have with him? Bandages, oil, wine, an animal for transport which meant he would have had to walk. Question: where did he get the bandages? Did he have a box of band-aids in his satchel? No. It is likely had to rip pieces of his clothing to bandage the wounds, of which there were probably quite a few. He took from himself to help a neighbor What if they were expensive designer garments? Would you tear yours to help a bleeding stranger? Would you give any of your physical resources to help someone you hardly know?

Ted Neeley is one of the greatest men I have ever known. When I started attending church regularly in high school, he picked me up on Sunday morning, Sunday evening, and Wednesday evenings and took me to church. He always had a couple more extras in his van. I never had to ask him for a ride. He would call fifteen minutes before he left to let me know to be ready and that he was on his way. This taxi service of his lasted for years. I didn't own my first car until I was nineteen. Mr. Ted's van rides are among my favorite memories of being in the youth group at church. He is a cancer survivor and has made numerous mission trips overseas and donates money to various ministries there. Mr. Ted is such a generous soul. Because of his kindness, I always offered people rides to church when I had wheels of my own. Granted, the comfort of Mr. Ted's van overshot my 1978 Honda Civic (don't judge me)!

My late pastor, Don Davis, used to frequently say, *People don't care how much you know until they know how much you care.* I am quite sure that saying originated elsewhere, but in this book, we will give the credit to him!

How have you cared for others? Have you helped someone with a ride this week? I realize we live in a society where it is not always safe to give rides to strangers. Do you have clothes sitting in your closet for a year or more that could help someone less fortunate? You learn that the family down the street have no couch to sit on. Do you have one you use less frequently that you could donate? Have you ever cooked a meal for a shut-in or for someone who has lost a loved one? Would you open your home as a church for those who have nowhere to go, or have been excluded from a church? When I say *you*, I am also saying *me*.

Remember that the Samaritan gave *after* he had compassion that compelled him to act. I believe if you and I can discover that Jesus level of compassion, we will give more than our share to help others.

Like the Samaritan, we will give regardless of racial, political, financial, or social status.

I'll say it again ... we are never more like Jesus than when we are giving our physical resources to help others. *For God so loved the world, He gave ...* (John 3:16). We should too.

A GENUINE NEIGHBOR GIVES OF THEIR FINANCIAL RESOURCES

Are you picking up on a trend in this story? Christian giving is always a response of some kind! The response is rooted in the fact that we have received first from God. This doesn't mean that we must repay God (as if we could). It does mean that our giving is genuinely and deeply motivated by gratitude. If guilt is your motivation, stop doing it. Come back to this parable.

The Samaritan took great care of the beaten man. He took him to an inn so the man could rest and recover. He gave the innkeeper the equivalent of the wages for two days of work. He then told the innkeeper, *if that isn't enough, I will pay you back for the extra when I return.*

A question I am often asked is, *how can a merciful, loving God allow children to starve?* I always turn the question back to them.

Philip Guedala, a nineteenth century biographer discovered that if you really want to find out how a person has truly lived, open their checkbook. For there, he says, you will find who they are and what they love.

Is it possible that children are starving because we pay $7.00 for a cup of coffee? Could it be that they are starving because we will pay over thirty-thousand dollars for a vehicle? What are you and I doing with the resources we have been blessed with? Are we giving it away, or are we wasting precious time griping because we don't have as much as someone else does?

Jesus asked the lawyer, *which of these three, do you think, proved to be a neighbor to the man who fell among the robbers?*

The lawyer answered, through gritted teeth, *the one who showed mercy.* Jesus told him, and I believe he is telling us, *Go and do likewise.* Actions speak much louder than words.

Reconstruction causes us to seriously think about our relationships with other humans. Who is our neighbor? Is it people who only look and act like us? Or is it everyone, regardless? Remember what that Samaritan did? Let's go and do that. Show up for people. When you are with someone, be present in the moment with them. Listen without formulating a response.

Actor, martial artist, and philosopher, the late Bruce Lee, once said, *"Real living is living for others."* If our reconstruction journey doesn't teach us to value others above ourselves, then we need to start again. That is what following Jesus is all about … living for others.

Part Three
THE RECONSTRUCTING

Chapter Eleven
CLEAN, CALLED, AND COMMISSIONED

> *"Let us then persevere unceasingly in our hope and in the pledge of our righteousness that is in Christ Jesus."*
>
> - POLYCARP OF SMYRNA

Of all the misinterpreted and misrepresented verses of Scripture, none stand out to me as much as Matthew 28:19-20, otherwise known as *The Great Commission:*

> "Go therefore and make disciples of all nations, baptizing them in the name of the Father and of the Son and of the Holy Spirit, teaching them to observe all that I have commanded you. And behold, I am with you always, to the end of the age."[27]

The phrase Great Commission is not found anywhere in these verses. It is not known exactly who coined the term Great Commission, but the phrase was made popular by famous 19th century British missionary Hudson Taylor, who spent 51 years on the mission field in China. For many years, missionary organizations have used the "go therefore," as the impetus for sending missionaries all over the world to share the gospel. There is nothing inherently wrong in this, but when we study the Great Commission in the original Greek, we

---

[27] English Standard Version

discover that the "go" is actually intentional. It should read, *as you go*. The "go" is not the imperative here. The command in the verse is, *make disciples*. Literally, *as you go, <u>make disciples</u>*. How does one make a disciple?

The word *disciple*, which is *mathētes* in Greek, literally means *pupil* but also *follower*, as in *Jesus follower*. What does a Jesus follower look like? Evangelically speaking, a Jesus follower is seen as one who blindly adheres to the teachings of the Bible. Young Christians are often taught that to be a true follower of Jesus, you must adhere to and obey his every command without question, as if Jesus were a drill sergeant and life was a test as to whether we get the text right. This type of following might work in the military, but not in the Kingdom of God. The idea of follower has a different connotation.

Followers are the actual persons who *implement* the ideas and strategies of a leader. They assist and accelerate the leader's vision to increase the effectiveness in the functioning of the organization. They are loyal to the leader and honest in their connections within the organization. Following Jesus is to implement his ideas and strategies like the Great Commission or the Greatest Commandment to love God and love others. Loyalty to Jesus is motivated by love and grace, and they work for the betterment of the Kingdom rather than selfish gain.

We have already investigated the lifestyle of valuing others above ourselves in chapter seven. Being a Jesus follower looks just like that. This doesn't mean that we stop thinking for ourselves. Each of us is uniquely created and we have within us the ability to change the world for the better. I can't do what you can do, nor the way only you can do it. No one can. That is your distinctive gift to the world! Jesus followers are invited to bring their creativity, passion, and talents into kingdom enterprise. We literally partner with Jesus through his holy spirit to share his love with the weak, the poor, and the marginalized. Having the mind of Christ,[28] we learn to think like him, love what he loves, and care about what he cares about. And we are not forced into it. It flows naturally from a grateful heart.

---

[28] 1 Corinthians 2:16

These facts and more are why it is amazing to follow Jesus.
But ...
There is another side to the Jesus follower coin.
It is a side that many followers fail to consider.

THE OPPORTUNITY COST OF BEING A JESUS FOLLOWER

In my early college days, I was majoring in Banking and Finance. I had a job at a local bank, and I thought I may as well grow where I was planted. Twelve years, three schools, three children, and two states later, I graduated with a degree in Biblical Studies. I made a few course corrections along the way. Dealing with other people's money lost its appeal early on.

One of my favorite classes back then was Macroeconomics. I learned the economic principle of *Opportunity Cost*. It is employed when there is a decision to be made. The formula for Opportunity Cost is *What you give up, divided by what you get in return*. In business, the formula can be useful and even insightful as you count the cost of an investment of your resources.

When it comes to following Jesus, there is a personal cost. It is an opportunity cost. I'm not asking you to sell everything you own and give it to the poor. Cost does not always apply to financial conditions. Opportunity cost compels us to weigh our options and consider our priorities given the situation. Following Jesus prompts a fierce evaluation of our personal priorities. *What is most important? What can I live without?* Consider an example from Jesus himself.

LUKE 9:57-62

> "Now it happened as they journeyed on the road, that someone said to Him, 'Lord, I will follow You wherever You go.' And Jesus said to him, 'Foxes have holes and birds of the air have nests, but the Son of Man has nowhere to lay His head.' Then He said to another, 'Follow Me.' But he said, 'Lord, let me first go and bury my father.' Jesus said to him, 'Let the dead bury their own dead, but you go and preach the kingdom of God.' And another also said, 'Lord, I will follow You, but let me first

go and bid them farewell who are at my house.' But Jesus said to him, 'No one, having put his hand to the plow, and looking back, is fit for the kingdom of God.'"[29]

FOLLOWING JESUS TAKES PRIORITY OVER PERSONAL COMFORT

Before I proceed any further, I want you to understand something. What I am going to share with you in this chapter has absolutely nothing to do with guilting or shaming you. The text appears that way on first glance, but there is so much grace built into everything Jesus says. I hope you know and believe that. Okay? Good. Let's jump in!

Jesus and his followers were traveling somewhere when some random person says to Jesus, *Lord, I will follow you wherever you go.* You would think that Jesus would love to hear something like that. Maybe he was. He responded to the person saying, basically, *Animals have places to live, and I don't even have an address of my own.* A common joke among preachers is, "What is Jesus' address? John 3:16." I never laughed either. As far as we know, Jesus traveled from place to place and depended on the kindness of strangers for food and bedding.

It is worth noting that Jesus answered the person. He could have brushed him off with a quip or ignored them completely. His answer may not have been the one he was expecting, but the Son of God took the time to respond to him! Jesus never turned away a sincere seeker. His answer to the man indicated that Jesus would love to have him as a follower, but that it's not going to be comfortable. He presented the man an opportunity cost. Here is what you give up over what you get. The man left. That was his answer.

There is nothing morally wrong with ministers who are very wealthy. Success and wealth are attainable for anyone if one is willing to work smart and take risks. Yet I wonder what these ministry moguls would say if Jesus said to them what he said to the man. I wonder if they would be willing to leave all of their wealth and comfort behind

---

[29] New King James Version

to follow Jesus. Would they gladly do so, or would they simply walk away like the man did? What would you or I do?

For the Jesus follower, personal comfort should not take priority over following him. That doesn't mean you necessarily have to walk away from everything you own.

Just be willing to.

FOLLOWING JESUS TAKES PRIORITY OVER PERSONAL POSSESSIONS

Jesus then reaches out to another person with this simple invitation, "Follow me." The person was willing to do it, he just had a request, "First, let me go and bury my father." Surely Jesus of all people would understand such a request.

In this near eastern culture, this is a figure of speech that referred to a son's responsibility to help in the family business until the father died and the inheritance was distributed. Failing to do this could result in a reduced inheritance or none at all. "Bury my father" really means, "Let me wait until I get what's coming to me, and then I will follow you." Let me get mine first, then you can have yours, Jesus.

In May of 1995, I surrendered to my calling to the ministry. I knew I had to prepare by finishing my education. I was accepted to Southeastern Baptist College in Wake Forest, NC. The plan was to move my family there as soon as possible so we could get settled in campus housing before classes began. During this time, I was approached by an acquaintance about this new multi-level marketing company she was representing. She recommended me, and I had the position before I even interviewed. It was moving too fast for me. I explained my calling to ministry and my plans to embark on the journey pretty quick. With great delight, she explained that she and her husband were going to be missionaries, but she wanted to make as much money as she could first, so they could serve without worrying about money.

Let me get mine first, then I will give you yours, Jesus.

What exactly is the problem here? Doesn't the Bible say to honor our father and mother? It seems like a reasonable request to bury one's father, right? Surely Jesus would support this request. Yes, but not as an excuse to delay your destiny and blessings as a Jesus follower.

We like to associate ourselves with Jesus by name, but too often prosperity becomes more important than being a Jesus follower. Remember when I mentioned that grace was built into everything Jesus said or did?

Jesus said, "Let the dead bury their own dead." Where is the grace in that statement? It is a gracious reminder that the world's issues do have their place of importance, but the Kingdom of God compels us to pursue a higher purpose. You and I are seated—present tense—in heavenly places with Jesus as joint heirs. Everything he has, we have. Everything he did, we can do.

I have learned many things over the years. One of those lessons is seeking daily bread. Jesus meets our needs every day. We are not looking for monthly or yearly bread. The future is not here yet. As for the past, there are only daily molded breadcrumbs. Personal possessions should not take priority over our positions as Jesus followers. You will have what you need.

The other person walked away. That was his answer.

FOLLOWING JESUS TAKES PRIORITY OVER PERSONAL RELATIONSHIPS

A third person spoke up. *I will follow you, but first let me go home and say goodbye to the guests in my home.* Again, a reasonable request. Hospitality was especially important to this culture. In the Old Testament, whenever strangers were guests in your home, nothing was too good for them. In fact, parts of the OT mention fathers offering their virgin daughters or sons to the guest as part of the hospitality. To not do this was a cultural *faux pas* that was inexcusable and could ruin one's reputation. To you and me, that is deplorable. In their time, it was socially acceptable and even expected.

Saying goodbye to his guests was right in line with this culture, however, it could take up to a year if done properly. Jesus knew that. He did not think badly of those who sought to follow him. Jesus was all about challenging motives. Knowing your culture and seeking to honor it is not evil. Jesus wants us to consider *why* we honor it. Who told us to honor our culture? Did God tell us, or was it our parents and grandparents?

It makes a little more sense then, when Jesus said, "Whoever puts his hand to the plow and looks back is not fit for the Kingdom of God." The man understood the reference. If you are plowing, you are trying to plow as straight a line as possible. Looking back would skew the line and you would have to pull back and start over. Have you ever tried to pull oxen in reverse? I can only imagine how hard that would be. Plowing requires full concentration. Especially that kind of plowing. Oxen are strong, but they are directionally challenged. That's why a man needs to drive the plow. Distractions create more work. More work takes more time that passes before you can plant. If you don't plant at just the right time, there will be little to no harvest. Without the harvest, your family will starve through the winter. Keeping your hand to the plow is for *your* benefit! The very things Jesus calls us to do are the things which benefit us the most!

Jesus was not saying, *you do not fit in the Kingdom like a square peg doesn't fit a round hole.* He is not calling us a misfit. He was making the point that following him is a forward motion. Looking back keeps you from moving forward in your spiritual life and as a Jesus follower. Therein lies the grace!

When we lose focus, or follow Jesus half-heartedly, we become less effective in helping others and magnifying the wonderful love of Jesus. As you read this chapter, ponder … is your spiritual life all that you need it to be? Is it all you want it to be? What is it that you need to consider giving up so you can move forward?

Let's visualize for a moment. Picture yourself living the spiritual life you want. Jesus and his grace are on full display in your life. So much so that others can physically see the spirit flowing through you. Isn't it wonderful? What you just visualized is so close!

What is holding you back today? Comfort? Possessions? Relationships? Take a priority inventory. What is most important to you? Why? Is it really that important?

Will what's holding you back have any eternal value or any kingdom value? Then why not let it go? Is it your theology? Your attitude? Your motivation? Are you stuck on *what's in it for me?* Deconstruction purges these things. Reconstruction helps you change your perspective on what really matters to you. Everything we release to be Jesus followers will be replaced with things so wonderful you will wonder how you ever lived without them!

Yes, there is a cost to becoming a follower of Jesus and fulfilling the Great Commission. Making disciples is about teaching them how to follow Jesus. What we discover in the process of reconstruction is that there is an even greater cost to putting your hand to the plow and looking back. Forgiven? Yes! Loved? Always! In the Kingdom of God? Forever! Grace and forgiveness are the power behind following Jesus. We can never lose it, so why not fully embrace your destiny, and become a world changer?

Let's go for it!

Chapter Twelve
THE GREAT COMMISSION CHRISTIAN

> *"Let us haste, let us run, my fellow men—us, who are God-loving and God-like images of the Word—let us haste, let us run, let us take his yoke, let us receive, to conduct us to immortality, the good charioteer of men. Let us love Christ."*
>
> – CLEMENT OF ALEXANDRIA A.D. 190

Evangelism has outlived its usefulness. I will say it again. *Evangelism has outlived its usefulness.* When I say *evangelism,* I am talking about the sales pitch. Maybe you've heard it before.

1. You have a problem. You are a sinner from birth. You are separated from God and his love. You are going to go to hell when you die.

2. There is a solution. Jesus died on the cross so you could be forgiven of your sins and go to heaven when you die.

3. You must act now. Pray the sinner's prayer. Join a Bible believing church. Get baptized by immersion. Start giving 10 percent of your gross income to the church.

There it is. The sales pitch. I could use this same outline to sell you insurance, a used car, or a vacuum cleaner. I could use this same formula to sell ice to Eskimos, and if I am convincing enough, they will buy it. Here's the best part, you don't even have to be a Jesus follower to pitch eternal life to others. You just need to be willing to share it with others on command.

Before you form a posse and grab the pitchforks, let me clarify my thoughts. From the time I became a follower of Jesus in 1983, my whole life has been about evangelism. Sharing the gospel. Winning the lost. Boycotting hell. Reaching the masses. Going into all the world. It was my "why" for many years. People who weren't "saved," or, "lost" people occupied my mind day and night. My youth group and I were on a mission to reach the lost. We started Bible studies at our schools. We invited our friends at school to come to church with us.

In college, I went on two short term mission trips. I attended meetings where we talked about ways to reach the lost. We talked strategy and purpose. The world must know Jesus! It must! And it was up to me to get the word out!

In my first two pastorates, I took members of my church family door to door in the neighborhoods surrounding the church building. We handed out gospel tracts and invited families to church. I led the church through FAITH evangelism training. We were going to be a Great Commission church if it cost me everything. It eventually did. I did everything I had been taught, and yet attendance was declining.

In my final pastorate, during a Church Council meeting, someone who didn't like me very much threw this gem out there.

"I don't think we are reaching people like we should."

I asked, "How should we be reaching people."

"Well, a lot of people think you should be getting more *porch time* in the neighborhood."

"Define porch time for me."

"Well, we think you're not leading us to reach people."

"Do you really need to be led in this? You were raised in church. You could probably teach me a thing or two."

Cue crickets chirping.

I continued, "Every time I have come to the church to suggest programs and enlist help in doing outreach, the Church Council (you) shoots every idea down. I would love to hear your suggestions."

At the next deacon's meeting, I was asked to resign. I was so relieved. My heart was no longer in it. I no longer believed in sales evangelism. After years of practice, I concluded once and for all that it did not work, nor did it honor God. People don't want you knocking on their door anymore. Therefore, I didn't want to do it anymore.

In 2002, Brian McLaren authored an amazing book on evangelism called, *More Ready Than You Realize: Evangelism as Dance in the Postmodern Matrix*. Basically, he reached the same conclusions I just mentioned about traditional evangelism long before I did. I discovered this book after I had written this chapter. I love Brian. He always says what we are all thinking before we even realize we are thinking it.

SO, WHAT IS A GREAT COMMISSION CHRISTIAN?

The greatest example for authentic evangelism is none other than Jesus himself, wouldn't you agree? Volumes of books have been written about the more effective ways of evangelizing. There is one story that stands out that best exemplifies a Great Commission Christian.

LUKE 19:1-10

"Jesus entered Jericho and made his way through the town. There was a man there named Zacchaeus. He was the chief tax collector in the region, and he had become extraordinarily rich. He tried to get a look at Jesus, but he was too short to see over the crowd. So, he ran ahead and climbed a sycamore-fig tree beside the road, for Jesus was going to pass that way.

When Jesus came by, he looked up at Zacchaeus and called him by name. 'Zacchaeus!' he said. 'Quick, come down! I must be a guest in your home today.'

Zacchaeus quickly climbed down and took Jesus to his house in great excitement and joy. But the people were displeased. 'He has gone to be the guest of a notorious sinner,' they grumbled.

Meanwhile, Zacchaeus stood before the Lord and said, 'I will give half my wealth to the poor, Lord, and if I have cheated people on their taxes, I will give them back four times as much!'

Jesus responded, 'Salvation has come to this home today, for this man has shown himself to be a true son of Abraham. For the Son of Man came to seek and save those who are lost.'"

THE GREAT COMMISSION CHRISTIAN INTERRUPTS THEIR JOURNEY

Are you close to the person who does your taxes? Moreover, would actually invite yourself into their home? Most of us would say no. Of course, if you do your own taxes, you will need to cut me some slack here!

Jesus, once again, is on the road. This time he is traveling through Jericho. A tax-collector named *Zacchaeus,* whose name ironically means *pure,* saw Jesus coming and wanted to get a better look at him as he was vertically challenged. Professionally, however, he was a *Chief* tax collector, and he made a lot of money at it.

While walking, Jesus stops and looks at Zacchaeus in the tree. He interrupted his journey. Whatever plans he had, were put on hold then and there. Authentic "evangelism" puts others above our plans and our agendas.

My brother, Jay, opened a coffee and espresso bar in Lexington, South Carolina a few years ago. He had just moved back from Seattle, and as a coffee enthusiast, wanted to bring some of that Seattle neighborhood coffeehouse charm to the south. He succeeded. I had the privilege of managing it for him. I was there nearly every day. Local churches really embraced Jamestown Coffee and spent hours there having Bible studies, or ministers having meetings. Sometimes after Wednesday services, people would stop in for some coffee-infused koinonia and stay until closing time. I enjoyed standing behind the counter and watching people enjoy our shop and our product. Jay had created something incredibly special in that community. It was one of the best jobs I had had in recent years. It didn't seem like work at all to me at all. It was fun!

I had just gone through a divorce and was not ministering anywhere at that time. I really enjoyed listening to the conversations between ministers and the cackling from the women's Bible study groups or book clubs. I was actually jealous of them all. I missed going to minister meetings and having Bible studies with a group. Here's the rub, though ...

The meetings almost always consisted of ways to better reach the communities. They discussed the latest outreach programs and how they were implementing them in their churches. At the same time, they treated our staff rudely. They complained about their coffee being too cold. But they did leave gospel tracts all over the place, even on the urinals, so there's that.

Are you seeing what I saw? They weren't willing to interrupt their important men and women of Gawd meetings about reaching people for Christ to show even a little kindness toward our people. Church youth groups were even worse, but then again, my old youth group didn't always leave the best impressions either.

Jesus interrupted his agenda for Zacchaeus to show us how to really reach people.

THE GREAT COMMISSION CHRISTIAN INITIATES THE RELATIONSHIP

In other places in the gospels, Jesus responded to those who called out to him. This is one of the only times we see Jesus initiating the contact. The story doesn't say that they knew each other, yet Jesus called him by name in the midst of a crowd of people. He knew Zacchaeus and reached out to him like a friend. He didn't ask who he was. He already knew. Jesus initiated the relationship with Zacchaeus.

My pastor and I meet for coffee every now and then when we can both make the time. I enjoy spending time with Kevin, and we always have the most amazing conversations. Sometimes I think I overwhelm him with my stories from the ministry, but he is a good sport and a great listener. He puts my need to share above his need to probably not want to hear it! That's the kind of man he is. He exhausts himself physically while reaching out to others and identifying their needs so he can try to meet them somehow.

One day we were meeting at our go-to Starbucks in West Columbia. It is right across the street from a busy hospital. We had been there about an hour and the conversation was winding down when we noticed a gentleman sitting by himself at the big table. He had his head in his hands and looked exhausted. He had a hospital bracelet on. He had obviously just been discharged from the hospital and walked across the busy road to the Starbucks. Kevin and I watched him for a bit and then Kevin just went and sat by him. He asked the man if he was okay and if he needed anything. Kevin ended up buying him some coffee, praying for the man, and giving him his business card and offering to drive him home.

We are often more comfortable waiting for someone to come to us with a need rather than going directly to them. Sometimes we feel that someone else will come along and care for them as we continue on our way. Kevin reached out. Jesus reached out. They initiated the relationship.

THE GREAT COMMISSION CHRISTIAN INITIATES CONNECTION INTO THEIR WORLD

Jesus didn't say to Zacchaeus, "Hey, shorty! Why are you in that tree?" He said, perhaps with urgency, "Quick, come down, I must be a guest in your home today." Not tomorrow. Today. Jesus didn't wait for the invitation. He invited himself into Zacchaeus' home. Culturally speaking, this was not the norm for hospitality. You get invited. You don't invite yourself. Why is that?

When you are in someone's home, you are literally in their world. You can see their magazines, the books on their shelves, the food in their fridge, the color of their carpets and walls, their personal hygiene, and the photos they display. You can tell a lot about a person by entering their home. Jesus invited himself into Zacchaeus's world. This was a big deal.

The flipside to this is that you can hide the things you don't want people to see if you know they are coming. I can recall times that I had guests coming and threw a bunch of things into the hall closet before they arrived. Perhaps that ridiculous collection of knick-knacks or the unsightly artwork your in-laws gave you for Christmas could be hidden until they actually come over.

Jesus invited himself into the personal world of Zacchaeus without giving him a chance to straighten up and hide the things he didn't wish Jesus to see. I have posed this question in many sermons, *is there anything in your "house" that you don't want Jesus to see?*

When Jesus poses that question directly to you, it is a lot more authentic. It's intense. Letting Jesus into your world … your whole world, is hard. But it is necessary. Reconstruction demands that we take inventory of our spiritual junk and throw some things away. It is a very refreshing experience to lay it all down at his feet. Zacchaeus had a blast doing it.

Without any prompting, Zacchaeus changed his life right then and there. Jesus saw him and his house exactly as they were. Instead of hiding, Zacchaeus came clean. He told Jesus he was going to repay all of the people he had stolen money from with interest and he offered half of his wealth. Jesus then proclaimed that salvation had come to that house, *for this man has shown himself to be a true son of Abraham. For the Son of Man came to seek and save those who are lost.*

The crowd was disgusted that Jesus invited himself into the home of a sinner. The worst kind of sinner in their eyes … a dishonest tax collector. You know how they feel. You work hard every week and yet your paycheck seems to get smaller and smaller. If Jesus were here right now and invited himself into the home of a corrupt IRS agent, we'd all be disgusted too. That disgust is one of those knick-knacks we try to hide when Jesus comes over.

What happened to Zacchaeus? Did he pray the sinner's prayer? Did he agree to join the local church? Did he walk the aisle and fill out the card? Was he baptized by immersion? The answer is *no* to all of the above, and yet Jesus proclaimed that salvation had come. What the actual heck happened?

Zacchaeus opened his home, his world, to Jesus. He hid nothing, ugly paintings, and all. He was open and honest with the Lord and with himself. Without one word of rebuke or criticism, or without a single note of an invitational hymn, Jesus declared Zacchaeus saved. You see, salvation isn't about getting your ducks in a row for Jesus so he will accept you. It's about letting him see you just as you are, unveiled and exposed. That is where he declares salvation over you. That is the good news! That is the gospel.

As you reconstruct your faith, I believe it is critical for you to visit this story again and again. We need the reminder of how loved, accepted, and affirmed we are. Jesus doesn't wait for us to get it together before he comes in. Jesus doesn't ask you to not be who you are before salvation can come. Open the door to your world and let him in.

Evangelism, reconstructed, is sharing this good news with the world. The Great Commission Christian doesn't even have to think about it. They are ready to share the love of Jesus with whoever they can. They don't need tracts or outlines. They are intimate and authentic as they share the love of Jesus with others. There is no need to force it. It just flows out of us. As Brian McLaren shared, evangelism should be as natural as dancing. You hear the music and you cannot help but move to it. When we realize that we are already loved and adored by Jesus, we can't help but be drawn into the music of the gospel ... the music of our salvation.

It is beautiful—and it is enough! You are enough!

Chapter Thirteen

SHEPHERDS, SHEEP, SOULS, AND SURGERIES

"I am like the sick sheep that strays from the rest of the flock. Unless the Good Shepherd takes me on His shoulders and carries me back to His fold, my steps will falter, and in the very effort of rising, my feet will give way."

— SAINT JEROME

A recent report showed that the suicide rate in America has increased 35% over the last two decades.[30] The suicide rate among Christians who attend church is significantly less, according to the *Wall Street Journal,* but it still happens. I have stared down that dark path twice in my life. Thankfully, I didn't go through with it. However, I do understand the level of despair and hopelessness involved in contemplating suicide. You search your heart and mind very deeply, and you cannot find one good reason to continue living. It is a black, empty, and helpless place in your mind.

Deconstruction can cause this if we're not careful. That's why so much of this book has been devoted to reconstruction. We are spiritual, divine people. Without a spiritual foundation, we are left with

---

[30] https://www.usnews.com/news/health-news/articles/2020-04-08/us-suicide-rate-climbed-35-37-in-two-decades

desolation and defeat. Sensing no connection to the divine leaves you feeling like a lamp that is not plugged in. You can switch it on and off all you want. If it's not plugged in, there will be no light. The same applies to our spiritual lives. If we are not plugged in to the divine source, there is no inner light.

The obvious dilemma here is that you want to plug in, you know you want to plug in, but you can't. You can't make yourself to connect to the source. You read books, listen to podcasts, and go to religious meetings and seminars. Nothing that used to work for you is working now. What do you do? What can you do? You're stuck in a spiritual slump and can't get out. You are so stuck, in fact, that unless God does something, you feel your life is over and there is nothing left to live for. What do you do?

What ... do ... you ... do?

Our answer lies in the 23rd Psalm.

> "The Lord is my shepherd; I shall not want. He makes me lie down in green pastures. He leads me beside still waters. *He restores my soul.* He leads me in paths of righteousness for his name's sake. Even though I walk through the valley of the shadow of death, I will fear no evil, for you are with me; your rod and your staff, they comfort me. You prepare a table before me in the presence of my enemies; you anoint my head with oil; my cup overflows. Surely goodness and mercy shall follow me all the days of my life, and I shall dwell in the house of the Lord forever."[31]

I would like to focus the remainder of this chapter on those beautiful words, *he restores my soul.* Psalm 23 is one of the most celebrated and quoted passages of Scripture. David wrote this Psalm while he was a shepherd boy. He understood the relationship between shepherds and their sheep and expresses it beautifully. He says that the Lord is his shepherd. The shepherd who provides for, cares for, and sustains us.

The relationship between a shepherd and their sheep is a unique one. It is a special calling. Shepherding, even today, is a twenty-four

---

[31] English Standard Version. Emphasis mine.

hour a day job. The shepherd eats while tending the flock. He sleeps close to them so he can be available right away in the event of wolves or other types of danger. The sheep are like his children. He knows them by name and the sheep recognize the shepherd's voice. Sound familiar? *My sheep hear my voice, and I know them, and they follow me. John 10:27.* The shepherd has a special bond and connection to the sheep. Why is this such a big deal?

With all respect to sheep, they are basically dumb animals. Without a shepherd to guide them to greener pastures, the sheep will stay in one place and eat all the grass. When they have finished the grass, the eat the stems. When they finish the stems, they eat the roots. After the roots are gone, they will continue to eat the dirt until they die. They are complacent animals. Complacency in our spiritual lives can be problematic and even stifling to our forward progress.

There is an expression among shepherds involving a *cast* sheep. A cast sheep is a sheep that has laid down and can't get up because its center of gravity is off—sometimes because it's pregnant or simply because it has a full fleece, or both. Once down, gasses start to build up in their abdomen and they can die in a matter of hours. If you get them back up on their feet, then they're fine. How does this happen?

A sheep who is full of fleece and expecting a newborn is a prized animal to the shepherd. The fleece will bring in good money, and the fact that the sheep is pregnant means they are productive, healthy, and strong. In this condition, sometimes the sheep needs to get more comfortable due to the extra weight. With one careless move, the weight shifts and before they realize what has happened, the sheep is flat on its back, and its legs go straight up into the air. The sheep can struggle, it can bleat, it can kick, but despite its best efforts, it cannot get vertical. Death will come in a matter of hours. The only hope for this sheep is that the shepherd will intervene.

Some years ago, a close friend of mine and I met for lunch. I noticed he wasn't his usual spritely self. He said, "Todd, the reason I asked you here today is that I want to tell you I am bankrupt." Not knowing what to say, I told him I came prepared to pay the check. He said, "No, I'm not financially bankrupt. I am spiritually bankrupt." I said, "What's going on with you? Tell me."

He explained that right now his life could not be better. He was soon to be married to his college sweetheart and had just been offered an important job in another city. By all outward appearances, he was living his best life.

Continuing, he indicated that his spiritual life was empty at best. He felt that his prayers were bouncing off the ceiling. He sat in church and felt nothing except a desire to leave. He said, and I quote, "I am flat on my back, spiritually, and I cannot get myself back up." Without realizing it, he admitted being a cast sheep. Unless God intervened, he was spiritually done for.

This, my dear friend, is where your spirituality gets real. When we come to the end of ourselves and what we know, we have nothing to grab onto to pull ourselves up. Oh, we can buy books, attend seminars, read the Bible more, pray more, go to church more, rededicate ourselves, make a plan to be more godly, go to counseling, buy a new devotional book, join an online Bible study, listen to Christian music, or join a monastery. However, the fact remains, unless God the Shepherd intervenes, we will remain flat on our backs.

The great news is that the shepherd does intervene. He runs over to the cast sheep to rescue it. The method of rescue, while remarkably effective, seems a bit harsh. The first thing the shepherd does is to remove the fleece—everything that gave that sheep its significance. First, he pulls out his shears and removes all of that wonderful fleece. Right there in the open field, he shears everything that made that sheep special.

Deconstruction feels like this. Suddenly everything that gave you your spiritual significance is gone. Like the sheep, you feel exposed and naked. Once all of that "fleece" has been stripped away, all that's left is you. The real you. The authentic you. All of your flaws are on display and there is nowhere to hide. That part of the process sounds awful.

It gets worse.

(Now I must employ a disclaimer here. What I am about to share next has been debated and debunked and debated again. Regardless, this practice is an ancient one and is no longer used).

The next thing the shepherd does is somewhat disturbing. The shepherd places both hands on the right front foreleg, and with a simple twist and pull breaks the leg of the sheep. This is done to restrict the animal from becoming cast again. It is done to save their life. To be frank, I thought it was cruel and unusual at first.

My first midlife crisis involved purchasing a used Harley-Davidson. I enjoyed riding it. Especially on sunny, spring days. After about 18 months, the thrill was gone, and I sold my Harley to a co-worker.

My second mid-life crisis is a bit more unorthodox.

During my second pastorate, I invited former NWA pro-wrestler Nikita Koloff to come and speak at our upcoming revival services. I've been a wrestling fan since I can remember. When I discovered that Nikita was doing full time ministry, I knew we had to have him at the church. I picked him up at the Charlotte, North Carolina airport and we had about ninety minutes together driving back. I sat there like a twelve-year old, listening to his old wrestling stories from the eighties. He talked about all of my favorites from that era, Ric Flair, Ricky Steamboat, Greg Valentine, Sting, and Dusty Rhodes. I also learned that his "uncle" and tag-team partner Ivan Koloff was also a Christian and doing ministry. I had the honor of introducing "Uncle Ivan" years later at a local wrestling show. The revival was incredible!

After the Nikita Koloff revival, I was looking for a way to use pro wrestling to share the gospel. I had no idea where to begin. To involve top tier stars like Nikita would cost thousands of dollars that neither I nor the church had. Sadly, not long after the Koloff revival, my marriage ended, and I was forced to resign. I had been stripped of the thing that made me significant: being Pastor Todd. Ministry was my life, and suddenly it was gone.

As I grieved, one day I received an email from a representative of a local Christian Pro Wrestling company. They traveled around putting on wrestling shows that concluded with an invitation to accept Jesus as their Lord and Savior. My prayers were answered! I reached out to the CEO, Timothy Blackmon. Today, he and I are dear friends. I asked about what they did and what was involved in having them come to our church. He sent me to their website, and that is where things took a weird turn.

I saw an invitation on their website that read, "Do *you* have what it takes to wrestle with us? We will train the right people!" Suddenly, I was twelve years old again and pretend wrestling with the kid next door and recalling how I dreamed of doing that one day.

I was in my early thirties when I saw the invitation, and I was in the best physical shape I had ever been in. A voice in my head said, *if you are going to do this, now is the time.* I called Timothy and he invited me to come and try out on the upcoming Saturday.

I took my kids and drove down to North Augusta, SC and met Timothy, who wrestled as "T-Money," and a bunch of the other incredible guys on the roster. My kids, especially Cody, laughed over and over as I was being body slammed, shoulder tackled, and clotheslined. He thought it was great!

The first thing I had to learn was how to "bump," or fall correctly onto the mat. If I couldn't bump properly, I couldn't wrestle. This was for my health and safety. After my first wrestling practice, I could barely drive home. I felt like I had been in a car accident. Everything hurt. Wrestling is not fake, believe me. It hurts! Still don't believe it? Stand on your porch or deck, facing backwards. Next, hurl yourself off and land on your back.[32] It is not fake, my friends, and should never be tried at home.

I went back every Saturday to practice with the guys. I was getting better, but not yet ready to be placed on the roster. One Saturday, I traveled with the group to a wrestling show in Branchville, SC. It was a beautiful little town and way off the beaten path.

After the ring was set up, we had a few hours before the show started. I asked if I could practice my bumping. Timothy paired me with a veteran wrestler, Dynamite Dave Kerr. He has wrestled for years and was actually once beaten with a leather strap by Chief

---

[32] Please, do *not* do this. You could permanently hurt yourself.

Wahoo MacDaniel ... on television. I was about to learn from one of the best. We were joined by another awesome WFJ wrestler, Nick Phoenix. Dave, Nick, and I are still great friends. Dave saw that I was struggling with bumping. He said he would show me how he had been taught. Nick Phoenix got on all fours behind me in the center of the ring, and Dave gave me a big push backwards. The very first thing you learn about bumping is that you *never* try to catch yourself with your hands. When Dave pushed me, however, I freaked out and instinctively reached out my right hand.

The next sound I heard was that of my radius and ulna shattering (not breaking) as my weight came down on it. I was in shock at first, and then I realized what had happened. Suddenly I was surrounded by concerned wrestling brothers trying to help. One of our security guys, Brian Gatch, was also an EMT. While we waited forty-five minutes for the ambulance to arrive, Brian held my arm in place the entire time. Dave felt awful. I assured him that we were cool and that it was clearly my fault. I felt so stupid and helpless lying there.

At once my thoughts turned to the cast sheep and the breaking of the right foreleg in order to save it. I was lying flat on my back, embarrassed, afraid, sad, and humiliated while Brian held my arm in place. Tears streamed down my cheeks. I was a cast sheep. I thought wrestling with a Christian company would give me back some of the ministry significance I had lost only months before. It didn't. I was cast. Stripped of everything, exposed in my weakness, and restricted for a season.

It took two surgeries to fix the arm. I have an eleven-inch scar there to remind me of that day in Branchville. The metal in my forearm is yet another reminder, especially when it rains. I did eventually heal and came back to wrestle with WFJ for a while. I "retired" in 2010. I was never a great wrestler anyway. I loved the experience though! I got to use my pastoral experience to help with the ministry side of the company. I also got to use my preacher voice as a ring announcer a bunch of times. That's how I was able to introduce Ivan Koloff. He was a guest speaker at one of our shows. He was a kind, gentle man compared to his "Russian Bear" persona. There was even a movie made about us, *Wrestling for Jesus: The Tale of T-Money*. I will never forget the friends I made and the experiences I had there.

The shepherd then restores the cast sheep. While the sheep is healing, it is carried by the shepherd for a time. The sheep's ear is deliberately placed over the heart of the shepherd. What a beautiful picture!

After a few weeks, the sheep regains its equilibrium and is able to return to the flock. Afterward, the sheep never leaves the shepherd's side.

The Lord is my Shepherd, and He restores my soul.

Reconstruction is very much a restoration of the soul. We lose all of our significance and unhealthy beliefs … the things that made us feel smug and important. We are empty, naked, exposed, and weak. It is here where we rediscover the real Jesus. Our shepherd who knows us by name, and we can hear his voice so clearly now that we are cast, broken, or deconstructed. Flat on our backs is a good place to be.

Healing begins.

    Refreshing begins.

        Restoration begins.

            Life begins again.

                But there will be scars.

My scar reminds me that God loves me too much to allow me to become full of myself like a cast sheep because I think I know better than Him. God didn't break my arm. I did it. I took it upon myself to regain what I had lost, and I found myself flat on my back literally and spiritually. I had no hope unless the Shepherd rescued me. Not only did he rescue me, he restored me. He reconstructed me.

Dear friends, he cannot wait to restore you! Abandon yourself to the love of our Shepherd and let him restore your soul! It might hurt a bit, but the restoration is worth it. Trust me!

Chapter Fourteen
THE VELVET JESUS PAINTING

*"If you never heal from what hurt you, then you'll
bleed on people who did not cut you."*

—NOTSALMON.COM

Reconstruction is *not* a guarantee that your life will be free of trouble. I've literally heard evangelists tell people, *just trust Jesus today and all of your problems will vanish.* If only life were that simple. I have coached with people who bought into that blatant lie. According to them, once they received Jesus as Lord and Savior, the excrement hit the winding metal, as it were. Freedom in Christ is not a free pass from life … it will continue to come at you. That's what it does. Sometimes it will come at you full-throttle and knock you on your hindquarters.

The difference is that having a reconstructed set of healthy beliefs and a fresh understanding of grace and peace gives you the strength not only to face life's challenges but to help others as life comes at them. When you don't have a solid foundation of faith beneath you, unexpected though inevitable life traumas can make you do things you never dreamed you could do.

Let me explain.

Years ago, I served as a volunteer police chaplain. I got to carry a chaplain badge and a pager for emergency calls. Once a week, I would bring donuts and hang around the station getting to know the officers. I would also do the occasional ride-along. I was also a pastor at the time. My ride along experiences gave me a very real perspective of what my local world was really like outside of the church walls. It was hard to see at times.

While I was still a chaplain, my pastorate was coming to an end. I was going through a personal crisis and my heart just wasn't in the ministry at the time. I still continued my work as a chaplain, though. It was a nice diversion and kept my ministerial boots on the ground.

One evening, I was home alone, watching TV. I received a page from the police station. The on-call chaplain was not available, and they needed someone to assist with a domestic violence call. Those were the worst, especially when children were involved. My job was usually to minister to the children. This call involved one small child. I had no idea what I was about to step into.

When I entered the home, I saw the child to my right, and the husband and wife were seated on the sofa, obviously smacked out of their minds. Above the sofa was a large velvet print of Jesus, probably bought at a flea market or roadside stand. It was beautiful. I remember thinking how different this home would be if they allowed the real Jesus into it. Suddenly things took a horrible turn for the worse.

While the wife was yelling incoherent obscenities at the husband, the husband reached underneath his cushion and pulled out a gun. As one of the officers yelled, *"Gun!"* the husband put the pistol in his mouth and pulled the trigger as the back of his head splattered all over the velvet Jesus. His head slumped forward, and it was as if someone turned on a faucet in his head as blood was just pouring out of his nose. Instinctively, I covered the child and took her outside. I was in shock. I had witnessed some harsh fights between couples. I helped chase a drug dealer one evening. I witnessed fourteen and fifteen-year old prostitutes get arrested. But I had never seen anything like this. Even the domestic violence I witnessed between my parents growing up was miniscule compared to what I had just watched.

In the span of about three months, I had had a great deal of personal loss. It was hard enough dealing with the major feelings associated with all of that. Now I had just witnessed a suicide that made absolutely no sense. The husband didn't even say anything. He was emotionless. The last thing I expected was for him to just shoot himself. I wondered if he hadn't been so high on drugs if that would even have happened. Was there anything I could have done to talk him out of it?

And what would become of the child—that poor little girl of about eighteen months old witnessed the entire thing and then saw her mother being taken away. She was confused and shaking as I held her outside of the home while the police did their thing. I was also confused and shaking. I wanted to speak to the little girl, but no words came out. Family services finally took the little girl, and I went home traumatized. The image of that man's brains splattering all over the velvet Jesus remains with me to this day. I did not sleep well for many months.

I turned in my chaplain credentials the next day. There was no coming back from that.

POST-TRAUMATIC-STRESS-DISORDER

More than 3 million cases of PTSD are diagnosed each year, according to the Mayo Clinic. It is a disorder in which a person has difficulty recovering after experiencing or witnessing a terrifying event. Mayo also reports that the condition may last months or years, with triggers that can bring back memories of the trauma accompanied by intense emotional and physical reactions. Symptoms may include nightmares or unwanted memories of the trauma, avoidance of situations that bring back memories of the trauma, heightened reactions, anxiety, or depressed mood.[33] It is treatable with medication and/or trauma-focused psychotherapy.

Symptoms of PTSD can be expressed through isolation. The affected person avoids contact with people as much as possible. Because we live in a society that teaches us to stifle our emotions, isolation only aggravates the onslaught of feelings since there is no one

---

33 https://www.mayoclinic.org/diseases-conditions/post-traumatic-stress-disorder/symptoms-causes/syc-20355967

to talk to. To compensate, individuals with PTSD turn to drugs and/ or alcohol to numb the mood swings. Those were the choices I made.

The PTSD caused me to have terrible mood swings. I wanted to be certain that when my children were with me, I could keep it under control, so I used opioids that I got from a friend. After a couple of years, the pills weren't enough. I started drinking on top of the pharmaceuticals. It became so bad, that I unapologetically drank in front of my children. They watched their loving father become a very dark person. Soon they stopped coming to see me and eventually broke off contact.

I went from job to job for a few years. I had no purpose or direction in life, except to get high or drunk. Usually both. I stayed in my apartment with the blinds closed. I seldom got together with friends, although I was being invited all the time. To appease my friends, I usually agreed to meet somewhere and then cancelled at the last minute.

Over a period of seven years, I had lost my family, my ministry, my home, and my car on top of the PTSD which I covered with substance abuse. I was barely hanging on to my faith in God. Other than my pets, I was alone. I was also toxic. I had alienated everyone that mattered to me. My years of avoiding my feelings and stuffing them way down into the black hole that was my soul had reached a point where even the drugs and alcohol were no longer helping with the pain.

ROCK BOTTOM, USA

Late one night in early 2011, I woke up and was freezing so bad I was shivering like an unbalanced washing machine. I thought I was going to die. Covered in five blankets, I began to talk to God.

"So, this is it, huh? After all I did for you, you're gonna let me die alone?"

I yelled and cursed at God for several minutes. All of my feelings came to the surface. I was sobbing uncontrollably. I could no longer hold it in. I felt every feeling that had been avoided and stuffed for so long. After denying Jesus three times, Peter sobbed. The Greek language paints the image of him literally vomiting tears. I felt like that. I cried, I screamed, I cursed, and I begged God to take me. I was like Lieutenant Dan in *Forrest Gump*.

I'm not sure how long my emotion dump and tirade lasted. I had nothing left in my heart. No more tears, no more emotions, no more profanity, no more talking at all. I was silent and the shivering had stopped. I realized I was still alive. It was here that I heard a still, small voice I had not heard in years. Almighty God, my Father, my Shepherd, spoke to my heart. He had never stopped speaking—I just wasn't listening. Now He had my complete attention.

"Todd, I want to remind you how much I love and adore you and how painful it was to watch you suffer. But ... "

Uh-oh.

"I want you to realize that you created all of these problems for yourself. I am not responsible. Your ex is not responsible nor are your children. You did this to yourself. You and no one else. I'm willing to help you now if you will allow me to."

I barely got the words out to respond.

"God ... help."

I was empty. All that could happen now is that I could be filled back up. I went to work the next day at the coffee shop. Emotionally, I was flat. I couldn't even fake being happy. Several regular customers asked me if I was okay. I said that I was just dealing with some personal stuff. My shift ended and I went home. I let my dogs out and made sure they had food and water, and then I went back to the shop and worked the evening shift. As manager, I was salaried, so I could work as much as I wanted.

That night, everything changed for me.

Laura walked into the shop. It was as if there was a spotlight shining on her as she walked to the counter. It was love at first sight for me, and I wasn't even looking for love. As toxic as I was, the last thing I needed was a relationship, much less a wife. Yet I somehow knew I would one day marry her. Laura wasn't as convinced as I was at first, but eventually she told me she loved me. She saved my life. She restored hope and happiness to me. She made me want to be a better man. Because of her, I reconciled with my children, got back into the ministry, and cleaned up my act. I didn't need the pills anymore. I had no desire to drink any alcoholic beverages. God helped me purge my emotional pit of toxic darkness so that Laura could come into my life. For the first time in an awfully long time, I was happy.

AVOIDING AND STUFFING

This chapter was written to encourage you to feel your feelings. I have coached with many people over the last few years who mostly have one thing in common: they avoid feeling their feelings and stuff them way down. Avoid and stuff. Avoid and stuff. Avoid and stuff. It leads to all kinds of addictive behavior, depression, anxiety, maybe even a kind of PTSD. When we work through their issues, breakthrough almost always comes when they get in touch with and identify their feelings. When I was in therapy, I learned a powerful coping skill known as *Opposite Action*. This skill has helped me many times. Here is how it works.

First, we identify the problem. Let's use loss of a job in this example. Second, we identify the usual way of coping unique to the person. It might look something like this:

1. **Identify the Problem**: You lost your job.

2. **Identify Your Feelings**: Fear, sadness, uncertainty.

3. **Identify Your Usual Coping Mechanism**: Get drunk.

4. **Next Usual Step**: Feel ashamed for getting drunk.

5. **Next Usual Step**: isolate, avoid, stuff, get drunk again.

6. **Result**: You're even more miserable than when you started.

We trace and observe each step until we reach the final result. In addition to the feelings associated with job loss, you have added shame, guilt, and isolation. Then we look at the situation again and do the exact *opposite* of what you just did.

1. **Identify the Problem**: You lost your job.

2. **Opposite Action Step**: Talk with someone about what happened to gain support.

3. **Next Opposite Action Step**: Do one productive thing like update your resume.

4. **Next Opposite Action Step**: Wake up early and start your job search.

5. **Result**: Organization, action, and managing emotions.

This coping strategy has helped so many of the people that I coach. The most important part of that strategy is identifying and feeling your feelings. If a person can at least do that, they are on the path toward healing. Two parts of our brain are affected negatively when we avoid and stuff our feelings and ignore them.

THE AMYGDALA

We mentioned the amygdala in Chapter Four. It is a small almond-shaped structure located deep in the middle of the temporal lobe in the front of the brain. The amygdala is designed to:

- Detect threats in the environment and activate the "fight or flight" response

- Activate the sympathetic nervous system to help you deal with the threat

- Help you store new emotional or threat-related memories

THE PREFRONTAL CORTEX (PFC)

The Prefrontal cortex is located in the frontal lobe just behind your forehead. The PFC is designed to:

- Regulate attention and awareness

- Make decisions about the best response to a situation
- Initiate conscious, voluntary behavior
- Determine the meaning and emotional significance of events
- Regulate emotions
- Inhibit or correct dysfunctional reactions

When your brain detects a negative circumstance, like the loss of a job, the amygdala initiates a quick, automatic defensive ("fight or flight") response involving the release of adrenaline, norepinephrine, and glucose to rev up your brain and body. Should the circumstance and related feelings continue, the amygdala communicates with the hypothalamus and pituitary gland to release cortisol. Meanwhile, the medial part of the prefrontal cortex consciously assesses the threat and either accentuates or calms down the "fight or flight" response.[34]

Emotional trauma causes lasting changes in the ventromedial prefrontal cortex region of the brain that is responsible for regulating the emotional responses triggered by the amygdala. The emotional trauma releases negative chemicals that can cause serious physical problems if prolonged. Opposite action and other effective coping skills cause the release of "feel good" chemicals. There are four primary chemicals in the brain that effect happiness: dopamine, oxytocin, serotonin, and endorphins. In their own way, these happy chemicals can become addictive, but in a good way. Imagine being addicted to happiness!

What is your velvet Jesus, that is, what is your PTSD trigger? How did it make you feel? Can you identify the different emotions? As you identify each one, make sure you feel that feeling. Talk to someone close to you about it. Pray about it. Meditate on the positives. Use mindfulness to examine your feelings without judgement.

The reconstructing of your mind involves getting in touch with the deepest parts of yourself. It compels you to face your demons, as it were. Reconstruction and restoration require us to revisit our velvet

---

[34] https://www.psychologytoday.com/us/blog/the-mindful-self-express/201809/how-ptsd-and-trauma-affect-your-brain-functioning

Jesus experiences and properly process them with therapy and possibly medication. Learning how to practice self-care is vital to the healing process. Talk with your doctor and identify physical issues such as sleep apnea. Failure to get regular sleep wears you down emotionally as well as physically. Correcting sleep issues could solve many problems for you. Decide what you need and get it. Take care of yourself. Be good to yourself. You're the only you that you have!

I often wonder what happened to that soiled velvet Jesus painting. Did they burn it or clean it? To help my healing process, I imagine that the painting was thoroughly cleaned and returned to its original velvet sheen, free of the stain of death.

Isn't that what the real Jesus does for us?

Chapter Fifteen
RECONSTRUCTING YOUR PERSONAL VISION

"When I dare to be powerful—to use my strength in the service of my vision, then it becomes less and less important whether I am afraid."

— AUDRE LORDE

I recall a *Peanuts* cartoon I read years ago. Charlie Brown, Linus, and Lucy are lying on the grass looking at the shapes of the clouds going by.

Lucy says, "When I look at that cloud shape, I think of man's constant struggle with good and evil."

Linus says, "That cloud makes me think of the *2nd Law of Thermodynamics*, which postulates that the universe is constantly closing in on itself. What do you see, Charlie Brown?"

Charlie Brown sheepishly responds, "Well … I was going to say I saw a duckie and a pony, but I don't think I will now."

Do you ever feel like the world is moving ahead without you? Are you only seeing duckies and ponies while it seems everyone else is seeing bigger things? Before deconstructing, I was perfectly clear who I was and what my purpose on this earth was. I was a Bible-thumping Baptist with a mission to preach the word and reach the world for Christ. That was my personal vision, and it was powerful. There is

THE RECONSTRUCTING OF YOUR MIND

incredible power in knowing who you are and what you are here to do. Maybe you can relate.

After deconstructing, I lost that power. I had no more vision of the big picture. I didn't know who I was anymore. I had no sense of purpose. Reconstruction gives us back what we lost. We realize who we *really* are and why we are *really* here. As Jesus followers, we are ministers of grace, healing, love, and justice for the weak. However, we may need to reconstruct our personal vision of how we use our unique gifts to present Jesus to the people in our world.

Where there is no vision, the people perish.[35] The Hebrew word *paw-rah'* means "to perish". *Paw-rah'* was the word used in a biblical proverb where a woman's hair was let flow out of its covering (hairband). Unconstrained in the wind, her hair is directionless and blown in all directions. Without a personal vision, we have no direction. We have no setting of our sails. The winds blow where they blow, and we can't control that. What we *can* control, in nautical terms, is how we set our sail. Setting the sail catches the wind and controls the direction of the craft. Having a personal vision is the setting of our sails. To set the sails, however, is not enough … we need to know what direction we are headed in. That is where reconstruction can add value to our journeys. We set our sails in a new direction. Then what?

I want to share three quick things about having a personal vision:

1. God has a vision just for you.

2. He wants to completely fulfill that vision.

3. He wants you to partner with Him in satisfying that vision!

I once listened to an evangelist who said that he always wanted to be an *impact player*. Some ministers, he said, were content to just hang out, do their jobs, and play it safe. That wasn't enough for him. He wanted to be involved in God-sized things. The reason, he shared, was that he had been an alcoholic literally living in the gutter. God delivered him from the big mess he had made of his life, and he wanted to

---

[35] Proverbs 29:18

honor that by having a vision that matched the depth of where he had come from. You may see things differently, and that is perfectly fine. There is an obscure and short passage from the Old Testament that illustrates the transforming power of a personal vision.

HABAKKUK 2:1-4

Habakkuk was a minor prophet who served in the temple. We will see him transform from a minor prophet to a major prophet because of a vision from God.[36] Habakkuk's name means *that which takes hold of or clings to some big idea*. He was serving in the temple at a time when God's people were refusing to hear His words. The first chapter of the story indicates that God was about to bring punishment to the Israelites. He was going to use a group of evil people know as the Chaldeans to accomplish this. The Chaldeans are also known as *Babylonians*. These were wicked and idolatrous people. Yes, God's people were wicked as well, but not as wicked as the Chaldeans. Habakkuk was flummoxed. He cried out:

> "O Lord my God, my Holy One, you who are eternal—surely you do not plan to wipe us out? O Lord, our Rock, you have sent these Chaldeans to correct us, to punish us for our many sins. But you are pure and cannot stand the sight of evil. Will you wink at their treachery? Should you be silent while the wicked swallow up people more righteous than they?"[37]

Some people believe that human beings should never question the ways of God. They may even feel that it borders on sin to ask God, 'Why?' But the book of Habakkuk is one of many places in the Bible that counters that idea. It is filled with a prophet's perplexing questions—and the Lord's penetrating answers. God never reproaches Habakkuk for asking two basic questions: Why does the Lord seem

---

[36] There is no substantive difference between a Major and a Minor Prophet. A true prophet can be defined as one who speaks only as the word of God comes to them. Major and Minor describe the length of the prophecy.

[37] Habakkuk 1:12-13

not to respond to the injustice and violence that Habakkuk sees around him? How could God use the vicious and idolatrous Babylonians to judge His own people? Habakkuk clearly had a beef with God. To his credit, he didn't waste time gossiping and complaining to others. He took his beef directly to God. Questioning God is not evil, my friend. Asking questions is what led you to deconstruction which led to reconstruction! Habakkuk was not afraid to challenge God, and neither should you be. Notice his determination to get answers.

> "I will climb up to my watchtower and stand at my guard post. There I will wait to see what the Lord says and how He will answer my complaint."[38]

What happened next is the springboard from where we will examine the power and impact of a personal vision.

THE CHARACTERISTICS OF A PERSONAL VISION

As we saw in verse one, the first characteristic of a vision is that it needs to be *requested*. Habakkuk went straight to God and asked him to explain why he was there at all. His job was to tell the people what merciful father God was saying. Now merciful Father God was about to unleash a brutal massacre and Habakkuk wanted answers.

Have you ever been vulnerable before God and asked him to show you why you are here? Moreover, have you committed yourself to remain until God answers your question? A desperate, sincere request from one of His children never goes unanswered. It may not come immediately—only God knows why—but the answers will come.

Moses was charged by God to lead the Israelites to the promised land. Along the way, the people of Israel whined, complained, and as we saw earlier, worshipped a golden calf. God told Moses that he was going to allow Moses to take the people to the promised land, but that He would send His angel with them instead of Himself. He was going to remove His presence.

---

[38] Habakkuk 2:1

In God's presence, hearts are mended, lives are changed, power is given, love is given. The presence of God kept the Israelites safe and empowered for the journey. Now God was going to take that away and sent an angel. Moses wouldn't accept that. He knew what was at stake. Notice what he did.

Moses went before God and challenged Him, basically saying that He has sent Moses to lead these people and now God was pulling out? The Bible says that God spoke to Moses as one speaks to a friend. If you can't ask a friend questions or challenge their decisions are you really friends? Following Moses' passionate request for God to stay with them, God agreed.[39]

Habakkuk went to God with his heartfelt request. Four hundred prophets were hiding in caves, but Habakkuk went before the Lord. Only God can *reveal* a vision. Only God has a vision for the future. Habakkuk wasn't afraid to ask God to include him in His vision, and we shouldn't be afraid either. With all of our flaws and shortcomings, God wants us to partner with Him. I have always taught my children that *it's how you finish that counts, not how you start.* As God's beloved, we desire to finish well.

In verse 2, we see the next characteristic of a personal vision is that it is *received*. The Lord answered Habakkuk. It became personal. Dear friend, you can be absolutely assured that the same God who answered Moses and Habakkuk will also answer you—personally. Not with some blanket platitudes or quippy church marquis. He will answer you personally as a friend. A friend who is closer than a brother.[40]

The vision should also be *recorded*. The Lord told Habakkuk to write the vision. Record the vision. Write it down so future generations can refer to it. Nearly every church or business today has a *vision statement*. The idea for that was likely inspired by Habakkuk 2:2. It is critical to write your vision down. Write it in a journal, write it on a word document. Frame it and display it proudly. When things

---

[39] Exodus 32-33

[40] Proverbs 18:24

happen or change, the vision statement keeps the boat anchored. It reminds us why we do what we do.

During the late 1990s, a friend of mine who pastored a large church in Tennessee was found dead in his study after he had taken his life. The congregation was devastated, of course. Certainly, they asked the question, *what do we do now?*

A renowned local church where many of my friends now go were faced with a scandal many years ago that rocked the church and the community. The pastor had confessed to an affair with the organist. This long-established church was nearly crippled by the humiliation. Surely, they also asked the question, *what do we do now?*

What did they do?

Both congregations recovered and moved forward. Want to know why? They both had vision statements. As tragic as the death of a pastor by suicide or an affair can be, the vision was written plainly to remind them why they were here.

THE COMPONENTS OF A PERSONAL VISION

The first component of a personal vision is *intimacy*. We discussed intimacy in an earlier chapter. Intimacy with God is where pain is mended, where miracles happen, and where visions are discovered. The intimacy needs to be ongoing, of course, and not just a one-time experience.

The next component is *imagination*. Some people insist that something must be seen in order to be believed. Jesus followers live by faith, meaning that something should be believed *before* it is seen.

How big is God? By this I mean is God big enough to fulfill God-sized visions in our 21st Century maelstrom of information? Of course He is! Then why should we be limited in our imagination as to what we can do in the Kingdom of God? Simple—we shouldn't. Ephesians 3:20 indicates that God can do exceedingly above what we can ask or think. In other words, so much more than we can imagine! I can imagine quite a bit, but God can do even more! The Law of

Attraction[41] teaches us that what we think about, we can bring about. How big is your imagination?

Reconstruction pushes the boundaries of our imaginations as we ponder the greatness of God, Jesus, and the universe. The possibilities can only be limited by our lack of imagination. What can you imagine? Do you have a big imagination? Many people do.

Bishop Wright was seated at the dinner table with his family one night and made the statement, "If God wanted us to fly, He would have given us wings!" His two sons, Orville, and Wilbur, would later prove that man can indeed fly.

It has been said that it's a shame that President John F. Kennedy didn't live to see man reach the moon. Actually, he did see it, and that's why it happened. He cast the vision and others saw it through.

Some say it's sad that Walt Disney didn't live to see Disney World and Epcot Center. Actually, he did see it, and that's why it was built. Disney had a large imagination and cast a large vision for his company.

I will ask again, *how big is your imagination?* Is it too big for God or this world? Your answer to this question can and will alter your life for the better, or for the worse. And with that, we come to the final component of a personal vision.

Transformation. Habakkuk was transformed from a "minor" prophet to a "major" prophet because of the personal vision God gave him. In verse 4, there is a curious but powerful statement, *the righteous shall live by faith.* This may have referred to Abraham in Genesis 15:6. In the context of our passage, God was comparing the attitudes of people living by pride or living by faith. This statement shows up again in the New Testament ... three times![42]

Two men returned home from a disappointing mission trip. They were despondent and believed their service to God was over because they had failed. While reading the Bible, they came across that statement, *the righteous shall live by faith.* This statement re-energized both

---

41   In my book, *The Renewing of Your Mind*, you will find more information about the LOA.

42   Romans 1:17; Galatians 3:11; Hebrews 10:38

John and Charles Wesley who went on to change the world and write some of the most well-known hymns of the faith.

Martin Luther was struggling to please God. He believed it was impossible to do so. He allegedly used to crawl up stairs to make his knees bleed in penance to God who was disgusted with him. Luther wouldn't even hold his head up because he thought he was unworthy of looking up at God. He was convinced that God would never love or accept him. While translating Scripture into German, he discovered *the righteous shall live by faith,* and the theology *Sola Fide (faith alone)* was born. Later, Luther would impact church history by spearheading the Great Reformation.

All of the above happened because God told a whiny minor prophet that the righteous shall live by faith in response to his request, and he wrote it down, not knowing the impact it would have.

Deconstruction challenged your basic beliefs just like Martin Luther's *96 Theses* challenged the religious elite and changed history. You are purging limiting beliefs. As you reconstruct, you will discover that no one or nothing can limit your belief and imagination about what you can do.

Conservative evangelical political American Christianity is talking about "duckies and ponies" with performance-based theology, problematic man-made rules, and ancient man-made traditions. Jesus followers need to know why they are here and what their place in God's Kingdom is.

You need to know.

You need to ask.

You need to listen.

You need to write it down.

You will magnify the real Jesus and change your world!

Can you imagine … ?

Will you imagine?

I can't wait to see the reconstructed you, sharing the love of Jesus and changing lives!

I imagine that Jesus can't wait either!

Parting Thoughts
WHERE DO WE GO FROM HERE?

Well, friend, we have reached the end of the book. I deeply hope that it meant something to you. Maybe at least one thing that you read will stick with you. Before I leave you, I want to offer some personal suggestions about next steps in your reconstruction expedition. You are not required to take any of them. As I said earlier, there is no blueprint. These are the things that helped me, though, and I want to share them with you. We have to start somewhere, right?

- I have stopped calling myself a Christian. For me, being a Christian today is more about politics, greed, comfort, and self-serving programs. I left all of that behind in 2016. In the years since I have discovered that there is so much more to being a Jesus follower. That's what I call myself now, by the way. *A Jesus Follower.* In the bigger religious picture, I guess I'm still technically a Christian. Day to day, though, I am a Jesus follower. Reconstruction signals us to question our identity as believers. It's really not about what you call yourself though. It's about being Jesus to the world.

- My wife and I are praying about opening our home to people who have been excluded for the Church in some way and need a group to belong to. Honestly, they could find a version of that at a local A.A. meeting. For now, I believe my focus needs to be on writing and podcasting. Take your time deciding what to do, if anything, about church. My church is sitting on my couch drinking coffee on Sunday. If you find a church family where you are comfortable, try it out. Give them a chance. Reconstructing your mind is a marathon and not a sprint. You don't want to rush right back into what you have already deconstructed from. God is wherever you need him to be.

- Consider looking outside of mainstream Christianity for a season. There is so much to learn! The experience of other religions can show us a great deal if we let it. God will not be mad if you do this. This also doesn't mean you have to convert; you're just learning, growing, and evolving. Studying other religions really helped me to become more grounded in my belief in Jesus and gave me some dear friends with different perspectives.

- Everything in the universe is hardwired with grace. It is built into everything you see and do. Make sure you give yourself plenty of it. Also make sure to give it away freely when you are out and about. So what if the person on the interstate cuts over and makes you hit your brakes? So what if the person ahead of you in the express lane has more than twenty items? So what? Share the love of Jesus until your heart overflows no matter how long it takes! Trust me, it gets easier and easier with practice, and there are so many physical benefits to easing up on yourself and everyone else. Grace and mercy are freely received and freely given.

- Finally, find others who understand what you're going through. I felt so alone after my deconstruction. I had no one to talk to about it, even my wife. She didn't understand all that was happening inside of me. One day I Googled *Progressive Christianity* and discovered an article by a guy named Keith Giles. Through Keith I have met so many like-minded people, most of whom are online. It is so odd, but many of my best friends, including Keith, are online and scattered all over the world. Most of us have never met in real life, but I don't know what I would do without them.

- Reading and listening to podcasts is a good practice since they are free of charge. There are also some wonderful teachings about deconstruction/reconstruction on YouTube. YouTube videos are also free. You only invest some of your time. Books may cost money but will be well worth the investment. You don't have to read every book, listen to every podcast, or watch every video. Find the ones that feed you and stick with them. Add more when you are ready. Use the list of books in the Appendix to start with. Take your time. There is no hurry to reconstruct your mind. It is a lifelong process, and as the old hymn says, truly, *every day with Jesus is sweeter than the day before!*

That's all I have for now, my friend. I hope that I have given you enough information to start building a solid foundation for your reconstruction. I am honored beyond words that you have chosen to read my book out of all the many wonderful books out there. If you would, please consider leaving me a review on Amazon and Goodreads.

Until then, my dear friend, may love surround you, may love flow from you, and may you forever be an instrument of love!

Namaste!

APPENDIX

- *A More Christlike God*, and anything by Brad Jersak
- *Apparent Faith, and The Tea Shop,* by Karl Forehand
- *Blue Like Jazz, and Scary Close,* by Donald Miller
- *Bringing Your Shadows Out of the Dark,* by Robert Augustus Masters
- *Edgewise,* by Jana Braden Greene
- *God Can't,* by Thomas Jay Oord
- *Jesus Unbound, Jesus Untangled, Jesus Unveiled,* and *Jesus Undefeated,* by Keith Giles
- *Out of Sorts,* by Sarah Bessey
- *Pastrix,* by Nadia Bolz-Weber
- *Searching for Sunday, and Faith Unraveled,* by the late Rachel Held Evans
- *The Renewing of Your Mind: Asking Modern Questions to Ancient Answers,* by Todd R. Vick

For more information about Todd R. Vick,
or to contact him for speaking engagements,
please visit *www.ToddRVick.net*

Many voices. One message.

Quoir is a boutique publisher
with a singular message: *Christ is all.*
Venture beyond your boundaries to discover Christ
in ways you never thought possible.

For more information, please visit
www.quoir.com

www.ingramcontent.com/pod-product-compliance
Lightning Source LLC
Chambersburg PA
CBHW050322120526
44592CB00014B/2014